ISLAM
and New Global Realities
The Roots of Islamic Fundamentalism

S.F. Fleming

Printed in Canada

Selah Publishing Group
Surprise, AZ 85374
www.selahbooks.com

Manuscript preparation:
Victropolis Creative Services
www.victropolis.com

ISBN 1-58930-061-0
Library of Congress Control Number: 2002103097

ACKNOWLEDGEMENTS

One month after the September 11th attack, I was contacted by the publisher and asked to write this book. Because of the sense of urgency and the critical time in which it was written, this book came together quickly. Yet, it would not have been possible without the great support I felt from all sides.

I thank my congregation for their prayers and encouragement. Mike Hunter and Yvonne Wayland and others immediately assisted me in finding information. Mike Croston, Brian Dockins, Andy and Kris West, took over responsibilities that I would have normally done. My secretary, Carole Krizenesky was of immeasurable support. My mother-in-law, Jill Jones, helped me so much by proofing another manuscript so that I could concentrate on this project.

I would also like to acknowledge the encouragement and information received from Pastor Ken Wilde of Capitol Christian Center in Boise, Idaho, as well as his associate pastor, Stan Kelly. Pastor Paul Tan of City Blessing Church in Claremont, California was kind to send me an article on Indonesia. Pastor Charles Harley of Liberty Church in Birmingham was very encouraging. I would like to thank my friend, Dr. Bill Hennessy, who wrote the foreword and sent me a useful article. Also, a big thanks to Ron Peck of Christian Ministry to Muslims for all the items he sent me.

Furthermore, I so appreciated the continual support of Garlen Jackson of Selah publishing and the help of all the support staff. Finally, I want to express gratitude to my wife, Kathleen, and my little girls, Susanna and Liberty, for being patient and understanding during these couple of months.

DEDICATION

This is dedicated to the saints at the House of the Lord, who have been so supportive!

CONTENTS

Part Four: Wrestling Against Principalities and Powers

FOREWORD

Recent events in the United States and Middle East have thrust the religion of Islam into the forefront of conversation around the globe. Experts have come out of the woodwork to explain to an incredulous world why a religion touted as a way of peace would endorse and even encourage the savage destruction of innocent people as a means of attaining Paradise for the suicidal perpetrators.

Even after months of public discussion, confusion persists. Perhaps the simplest explanation for the rise of Islamic militant behavior comes from the understanding that *Islam* doesn't mean "peace." It is more accurately translated "submission."

Islam doesn't promote an ordinary submission. Rather, it is submission to an unknowable god who demands complete obedience without offering the individual follower the luxury of discerning his will. So the followers of Allah turn to religious teachers who function as interpreters of Allah's will. Many times tremendous license is granted to Islamic teachers without real accountability. Unscrupulous teachers can sometimes combine the words of Muhammad with the devotion of sincere Muslims to advance their own personal or political agenda. The results can be disastrous.

Having spent a number of years in Africa, I witnessed extreme discomfort of Muslims living in a society where the teachings of Islam and the gospel of Christ were presented side by side. It was inconceivable to Islamic leaders that individuals might be given the option of choosing between Islam and Christianity.

In my experience in planting churches in Northern Nigeria, the power of the Gospel to introduce people to a God who desired to be known often overcame the fear motivating devotion to an unknowable Allah. In other words, many Muslims will come to Christ if only they hear His message.

This book promises to serve as a valuable tool providing the reader with an accurate understanding of Islamic teachings. Hopefully, it will motivate Christians to both pray and respond to the challenge of living for Christ in a changing world. The Church must understand and confront Islam. It continues to be one of the fastest growing religions in the United States and Europe.

My personal prayer is that through reading this book (1) every reader will discern God's deep desire, (2) the life-changing message of Jesus Christ will penetrate every corner of our world, and (3) the reader will be convinced of God's relentless desire to seek and to save those who are lost.

—Dr. Bill Hennessy
Cape Town, South Africa

PART ONE

THE MODERN ISLAMIC CRISIS

✡ ✞ ☪

CHAPTER 1

ATTACK ON AMERICA

Setting: The fortress at Alamut in the Elburs Mountains, south of the Caspian Sea, AD *1122.*

The Islamic terrorists known as the *fida'iyun* stood at attention. Each rank silently weighed the words of their leader, Hasan as-Sabbah, as he described the plan of attack. Years of running, killing, and attacking the political enemies of Allah had hardened Hasan and his men to the extreme dangers of the missions. So there was a brief pause when Hasan noted fear in the eyes of Muhammad, a new Egyptian recruit.

The assassination of Seljuq Vizier Nizam al-Mulk would not be easy. He was one of the most protected people in the world. Regardless, he was crippling terrorist cells around the Mediterranean, in Egypt, in southeast Iran, and even at this mountain fortress south of the Caspian Sea. Hasan continued pacing in front of the men, but he held their gaze with his while ensuring they understood that Al-Mulk could no longer be allowed to interfere in the expansion of Allah's Islamic kingdom.

Muhammad's mind wondered. He could hear his grandmother again, just a few months ago, asking him not to join the ranks of Hasan, the "old man from the mountains." She explained that Allah's ways were peaceful. Of course, what did she know about what was happening in the world? Times were changing. Important things were happening to secure the kingdom of Allah. Perhaps he would be asked to do a very important mission; one that would bring glory to Allah.

"Assassins for Allah!" Hasan barked. Muhammad snapped back to reality.

Hasan was holding up a copy of the Koran while fire lit his eyes. "Why are you called the *fida'iyun*?"

They responded as one: "Because we are ready to sacrifice our lives for Allah and his Prophet. There is no god but Allah, and Muhammad is Allah's Prophet!" It was as loud and clear as they had yelled it a thousand times before.

Hasan stood tall and waived the Koran over them. "Believers! Wage war against such of the infidels as are your neighbors, and let them find you rigorous; and know that God is with those who fear him. Kill those who join other gods with God wherever you shall find them, and lay wait for them with every kind of ambush."

Great shouts went up by all the assassins, some praising Allah, some swearing upon their souls to kill Allah's enemies, and some cursing the name of Nizam al-Mulk. Others were talking about the instant glories of heaven that would be given to any who died for Allah in the fight.

A wisp of a smile crossed Hasan's lips. He was pleased with his motivational speech. Even Muhammad's face had changed, growing in resolve with the volume of shouts for a holy jihad by all terrorists against all lands and people who oppose sacred Islam. *Now, they are almost ready. This attack will be special—a suicide mission. Let's see who will volunteer for the glory of Allah.*

He snapped them back to attention. Then he said to the young Egyptian, "Go into the other room and get the hashish. We will enjoy the moment, and then we shall all talk some more."

Where were you on September 11, 2001? Many people can tell you exactly what they were doing at the moment they learned about the attack on the World Trade Center and the Pentagon. Workers around the world dropped their tools. Businessmen left their desks. Parents picked up their children from schools. The freeways emptied. People cancelled plans and braced for the unknown. Billions stared in disbelief at televisions or leaned close to radios to learn of the terrifying events that unfolded across the airwaves. The plot was diabolical yet sickeningly compelling.[1]

- 8:45 A.M., American Airlines Flight 11, out of Boston, Massachusetts, crashed into the north tower of the World Trade Center with 92 people on board.
- 9:03 A.M., United Airlines Flight 175 crashes into the south tower with a total of 65 passengers and crew.
- 9:43 A.M., American Airlines Flight 77, carrying 64 people, crashes into the Pentagon. One of the building's five sides collapses.
- 10:05 A.M., the south tower of the World Trade Center collapses.
- 10:10 A.M., United Flight 93 crashes in Somerset County, Pennsylvania, killing 45.
- 10:28 A.M., the north tower of the World Trade Center collapses.

Emotions of grief, fear, and anger erupted around the dust clouds of New York. Airplanes as bombs? Hijackers with cardboard cutters? Trained in the United States? How many thousands are buried in the rubble?

There was a massive rush of rescue units to ground zero in New York and Washington, D.C. Financial markets closed. Switchboards were jammed as families tried to learn what had become of their loved ones. For the first time in aviation history, the skies were cleared of all air traffic. Government leaders bunkered themselves in war rooms and secret locations to strategize. Talk shows and news programs dropped commercials and stayed on the air 24 hours a day, fitting the new pieces of information into the growing puzzle.

There are over 1.2 billion Muslims, which is 20% of the world's population.

Across the country, Americans began to pray. Churches were packed with new faces that reflected shock, confusion, and worry. During the National Day of Prayer and Mourning at the Washington National Cathedral, heads of state, along with President Bush, the Reverend Dr. Billy Graham, and people of many faiths—including Muslims—came together to comfort the nation and mourn.

Around the globe, heartfelt condolences poured in for the victims together with stern condemnation for the "evildoers." Israel's prime minister, Ariel Sharon, declared a day of mourning on behalf of the United States. Japan asked its citizens to pray. Pastors in Russia called for a day of prayer for America.[2] Scores of countries grieved on behalf of America and offered assistance and political support.

Yet, in many Islamic countries, shouts of joy were heard, along with praises to Allah for the attackers' success. Guns were fired in the air. The older generations clapped their hands in celebration and threw candy to children.

Why? How could they celebrate so much grief?

In the days following September 11th, good answers were hard to find. Misinformed opinions seemed to multiply in the wake of the crisis. A radio talk-show host discussed with callers whether or not Ishmael was really the thirteenth tribe of Israel. He wasn't sure. Other programs suggested that Allah is simply another name for the God of the Jews and the Christians. The jihad concept was a hot topic, but many Muslims disagreed whether or not it was a valid part of their faith.

Prominent leaders tried to dissuade vigilantes against targeting American Muslims. But in the land of religious freedom, Arab minority groups were quickly singled out. Impulsive individuals became convinced that all Arabs are Muslims and all Muslims are anti-American. A car rammed a Mosque in Cleveland. An Iraqi-owned restaurant in Massachusetts was torched. A man wearing a turban was shot and killed at a gas station in Arizona. There were over 800 incidents in the first month after the attack on America.[3] Immigrants and foreigners from Arab nations stayed indoors.

Every time the number of Muslims in the United States was estimated, the total grew larger. One gentleman, who represented a government agency that hopes to promote tolerance and a sense of commonality, claimed there were 15 million Muslims in the United States. The actual number based on the 2000 edition of the annual *Yearbook of American and Canadian Churches* estimates that 3,950,000 Muslims live in America. In 1999, the American Muslim Council estimated an optimistic 6.5 million.[4] It's safe to assume there are between 5 and 6 million.

Rumors also circulated after the attack. One declared 4,000 Jews who worked in the devastated area had been informed to stay home on September 11.[5] The Arabic media touted this as proof that Israel, rather than Islamic fundamentalists, was actually behind the attack. In truth, many Jews died in the tragedy.

The U.S.-led war on terrorism in Afghanistan did not eliminate the anxieties, but it allowed many people to refocus their energy into a renewed sense of patriotism. During one raid on a Taliban-owned house in Afghanistan, a video was discovered that showed Osama bin Laden, the prime suspect of the September attack and leader of the al-Qaeda terrorist network, joyfully recounting the event. The transcript reveals how he had planned to spill the blood of many.

> OSAMA BIN LADEN: We calculated in advance the number of casualties from the enemy who would be killed based on the position of the tower. We calculated that the floors that would be hit would be three or four floors. I was the most optimistic of them all. . . . Due to my experience in this field, I was thinking that the fire from the gas in the plane would melt the iron structure of the building and collapse the area where the plane hit and all the floors above it only. This is all that we had hoped for.

Osama received more than he hoped for. Thousands died. Ever since that day, Americans have suffered from an increased fear of flying and have been learning to cope with new threats, like biological warfare, economic upheavals, and the nagging uncertainty that any neighborhood could be home to dangerous terrorists. In contrast, Osama bin Laden considered it a success:

> OSAMA BIN LADEN: This event made people think [about true Islam], which benefited Islam greatly.

Also interesting is how Osama bin Laden relied on the Koran, the primary Islamic holy book, to defend his violent actions:

> OSAMA BIN LADEN: [quoting the Koran] "I was ordered to fight the people until they say there is no god but Allah, and his prophet

> Muhammad." "Some people may ask: why do you want to fight us?" "There is an association between those who say: I believe in one god and Muhammad is his prophet, and those who don't."

Another individual in the video, a sheik who had come to congratulate Osama, reflected on the attack as a *jihad*, a holy war that benefits Islam.

> SHEIK: . . . This is the guidance of Allah and the blessed fruit of jihad. . . .

Are these perspectives representative of Islam worldwide? Not entirely. Yet throughout Islam's history, aggression has been a key to spreading its influence. The word *Islam* means "submission." Even from the first years of Mohammad, this religion has offered prospective converts a *unique* alternative: submission or death.

After the attack, many questions continued to ricochet:

- "Why did they attack us?"
- "Are Muslims peaceful or violent?"
- "Are all Arabs Muslims?"
- "Why do they call us the Great Satan?"
- "Is Osama bin Laden a true Muslim or just a fanatic?"
- "Is a *jihad* (holy war) real, or is it something that was made up for movies?"

The information compiled in this volume will attempt to answer such questions and provide a better understanding of Islam, its goals, and how Christians can make a positive difference.

CHAPTER 2

OSAMA BIN LADEN AND MODERN ISLAMIC FUNDAMENTALISM

Setting: Afghanistan, the year 2000.

High atop the Hindu Kush Mountains, Osama scanned the windswept and dusty valleys of Afghanistan until his eyes fell on Kabul. The diversity of the terrain had lulled him deep into thought until he heard the door close on a jeep. Gravel footsteps drew closer until Omar stood by his side, using both hands to shade his one eye from the sun and wind.

"Osama, do you know the mythical story about how Allah made Afghanistan?"

Osama answered casually, just above the blare of the wind, "No."

"After Allah made the rest of the world, he had a lot of rubbish. There were strange pieces that didn't fit anywhere else. He gathered them together and threw them here."

"Is that how Satan ended up in Kabul?"

"If the legend is true, perhaps Allah threw him out of paradise with the trash. . . . Of course, prior to Cain starting the city."

Osama's eyes narrowed. "If Satan is here, we must throw him out and establish the law that honors Allah."

"No one wants that more than me." Omar scanned the horizon. "We ran the Russian dogs out along with the uncommitted Mujahideen. Our battle scars testify of courage and dedication. We will protect this land."

Osama turned and caught Omar's eye. "Even against the Americans?"

"Allah's will be done. He destroyed the Russians, and He will obliterate the Americans should they ever invade this country."

Prior to September 11, 2001, Osama bin Laden was not important to the average American. After the attack, he was instantly the most wanted terrorist in the world. Believed to have been involved in the killings of thousands, here are a few of his career highlights:

- The killings of Western tourists by Islamic militant groups in Egypt
- Bombings in France
- 1992 bombings of a hotel in Yemen
- 1993 World Trade Center bombing, killing 6 and wounding hundreds
- 1995 detonation of a truck bomb in Riyadh, Saudi Arabia, killing 7
- 1995 assassination attempt on Egyptian President Hosni Mubarak
- 1996 truck bomb in Dhahran, Saudi Arabia, killing 19 U.S. servicemen
- 1998 bombing of the U.S. embassies in Nairobi, Kenya, and Dar-es-Salaam, Tanzania, killing 224 people

- October 2000 attack on the U. S. destroyer ship Cole in Yemen, killing 17 U.S. servicemen[1]
- September 11th, 2001, attack on the World Trade Center and the Pentagon

In May 1998, ABC News correspondent John Miller interviewed Osama bin Laden. In the closing comments, Osama made his motivations clear:

> We are worshipers of Allah and we carry out our duties. Our duty is to call on all nations to join the light. Our first duty is being people of this religion and to fight for this religion. . . .

Osama bin Laden justifies his violence as a reasonable tool for the spread of Islam, which is a common thread throughout Islamic fundamentalism. Unfortunately, capturing Osama would not end terrorism. There are many like him throughout the world, but he is an outspoken member of his movement. A look at his life and words may bring additional understanding to the ideology that drives this movement.

Osama was born in 1957, the seventeenth son of more than fifty children of Mohammed Awad bin Laden, a Yemeni who owned the leading construction company in Saudi Arabia. Osama inherited millions of dollars after his father died. At age 17, Osama married a Syrian cousin and then attended King Abdul Aziz University in Jidda. One of his teachers was Abdullah Azzam, a Palestinian who played a large role in the resurgence of Islamic fundamentalism.[2]

In 1979, Osama raised money for the Mujahideen, the Muslim guerrilla warriors who fought the Soviets in Afghanistan. In the mid 1980s, he built training camps to further the cause. His connections eventually led him to numerous Islamic extremist groups, like the Egyptian Islamic Jihad. Once his mind was set on expanding the battle toward the West, it was an easy step to turn his military training camps into staging centers for worldwide terrorism.

In 1988, he formed the Al-Qaeda terrorist network, which dispersed thousands of militant recruits from the Middle East into over 50 different countries. Ten years later, Osama was instrumental in the formation of the International Islamic Front for Jihad Against Jews and Crusaders, an umbrella group of Muslim militants unified in their religious duty to kill Americans anywhere possible.

The Gulf War in the early 1990s brought American soldiers into Saudi Arabia, the sacred home of the prophet Muhammad and Islamic holy city of Mecca. Osama publicly opposed the decision of the Saudi king to allow the infidels to have bases there. After losing Saudi citizenship in 1994, he moved to Sudan. Two years later, he relocated to Afghanistan and became heavily involved with the Taliban, a growing fundamentalist group.[3]

The Taliban was a Mujahideen faction that emerged in 1989 to fight against the Afghani central government. The name *Taliban* means "student," implying that members were students of the Islamic religion. Led by Mohammad Omar, these people studied war most of their lives.

In 2001, reports surfaced of two significant events for Osama, including "a three-day terrorist convention of sorts held earlier this year in Beirut," where "Mr. bin Laden's Al-Qaeda organization joined forces with Hamas, Islamic Jihad, and Hezbollah to pledge themselves to joint jihad, or holy war. Their immediate aim: the destruction of Israel."[4] Obviously, the United States, due to their support of Israel, was also a target of these terrorist groups.

The second event pertained to Osama's son, Mohammad bin Laden, who married the daughter of Mohammed Atef, a member of the Egyptian Islamic Jihad. This band of extremists was best known for its 1981 assassination of Anwar Sadat. "The simple wedding this year was more than a union of two families. It heralded the fusion of two of the world's top terror organizations. The merger has transformed Al-Qaeda, fostering new discipline among a loose association of terrorist organizations from more than 60 countries."[5]

The Rise of Islamic Fundamentalism

The Islamic worldview is rooted in two things:

1. Muhammad, the seventh century prophet of Islam
2. Koran, a collection of revelations Muhammad claims he received from Allah

The rise of fanatical terrorists and their coalitions have brought Islamic fundamentalism to a new form. This has resulted in great conflict within Islam.

Modern Islamic fundamentalism may have originated with a group known as the Muslim Brotherhood. This organization, founded in Egypt in 1928 by its teacher, Hasan al-Banna, gained support from many Arabs who were dissatisfied with the results of the 1919 national revolution. The Muslim Brotherhood reacted negatively to the "British hegemony and more generally against the modernization of the country on a Western model. In order to end the supremacy of European states over Arabs, the movement summoned its followers to *jihad*. Its main demand: Return to an Islamic state and to a social order stringently oriented toward the Koran and Hadith."[6] Both are holy books to Islam.

Is fundamentalism unique to Islam? In her book, *Islam: A Short History*, Karen Armstrong, one of the world's foremost scholars on religious affairs, assures us that it is not:

> The Western media often give the impression that the embattled and occasionally violent form of religiosity known as "fundamentalism" is a purely Islamic phenomenon. This is not the case.

> Fundamentalism is a global fact and has surfaced in every major faith in response to the problems of our modernity. There is fundamentalist Judaism, fundamentalist Christianity, fundamentalist Hinduism, fundamentalist Buddhism, fundamentalist Sikhism, and even fundamentalist Confucianism.[7]

Not everyone likes the term *fundamentalism* for Islam. For instance, John L. Esposito, the author of *Islamic Threat: Myth or Reality?* prefers the terms *Islamic revivalism* or *Islamic activism* instead:

> First, all those who call for a return to foundational beliefs or the *fundamentals* of a religion may be called fundamentalists . . . Second, our understanding and perceptions of fundamentalism are heavily influenced by American Protestantism . . . For many liberal or mainline Christians, "fundamentalism" is pejorative or derogatory . . . Third, 'fundamentalism' is often equated with political activism, extremism, fanaticism, terrorism, and anti-Americanism . . . Yet, while some engage in radical religiopolitics, most . . . work within the established order.[8]

However unfair the term may be, *fundamentalism* has become the common vernacular for many movements.

Although, the majority of the Islamic world is deeply opposed to the surging influence of fundamentalists, "The sense that Islam is under siege is quite widespread, even among moderate Muslims, who have condemned the recent terrorism."[9] Also, John Esposito says that the majority of so-called fundamentalist organizations function effectively within the political system "because they are urban-based, led by well-educated leaders who attract students and educated followers, are well placed in the professions (engineering, science, medicine, law, education, the military), and organizations provide social and medical services."[10]

More Than Politics

Islamic terrorist regimes wreak havoc on every inhabited continent of the world. Until now, it seemed as though Osama's main goals were religious, rather than political. For instance, in 2001 Islamic militants with the organization Abu Sayyaf ("bearer of the sword"), which has links to Osama bin Laden, kidnapped Christian missionaries in the Philippines. They wanted to send a clear message: "Stay out of the southern Philippines," a predominantly Muslim territory. Indonesia, home to the largest population of Muslims in the world, is currently persecuting thousands of Christians. The whole affair has caused troublesome questions to arise within the Muslim religion.

Islam is the second largest world religion behind Christianity.

After the attack on 9/11/01, many Muslims ran for cover, not wanting their religious doctrine to be associated with the tragedy. They claimed Islam was a peaceful religion, so the whole thing had to have been a mistake. Yet, many refused to discuss terrorism in light of the historical use of aggression in Islamic doctrine.

During a special CNN report on Islam, an American imam (leader of a Muslim congregation) preached to his flock about the horrific attack on America. "It was not Islam. I want to mention that to you. It is no way, no form, or fashion identified with Islam. That [which] happened in New York was not Islam."[11]

Peaceful religious leaders often label Islamic fundamentalist groups as cults. But is that accurate? The fundamentalist network has many followers, is condoned by political factions of the Middle East and Africa, and its religious interpretations seem to be gaining approval, especially the use of aggression to spread its religious and political influence. One example from a 200-page training manual captured from the terrorist network calls for the "overthrow of godless regimes" by "blasting and destroying the embassies and attacking vital economic centers."[12]

There is also the issue that Islamic fundamentalism is growing and influencing the future leaders of Islam. Osama bin Laden's worldview is central to a new generation of religious schools. One headmaster who was interviewed said, "The use of force is permitted where there is oppression, like in countries where Muslims begin to loose power. God Almighty has created the iron. With iron we can create guns. So when there is unimaginable oppression in the world it is permitted to take up arms." In regard to support of what bin Laden and terrorists had done, he said, "Here in this mosque, as elsewhere, we pray for him."[13]

Traditionally, Islamic teachers claim the Koran forbids suicide. Yet, within the Hezbollah (Lebanese Party of God Movement), suicide bombers are trained in military ranks with mock bombs strapped to their bodies. Members regard "self-martyrdom" as the only way to fight back. They practice terrorist maneuvers that will put them within close proximity of Israeli personnel and armored vehicles before pulling the pin. One man defended the practice by saying, "They don't consider it suicide, because they value their life."

The Hezbollah exalts these individuals by hanging their pictures on city streets, with startling effect. One little boy said he wanted to be a martyr just like his father, in order to "kill our Zionist enemy and drive them out of our land." Another man, only twenty years old, was heralded after blowing himself up with Israeli soldiers. In a video message to his family, he instructed them to receive congratulations rather than condolences.

The World Islamic Front

Osama bin Laden and his network manifest hostile actions toward the West in response to the perceived threat on their religion. The Islamic fundamentalist movement has awakened a growing and intense hatred toward the United States that is hard for some Western minds to understand.

On February 3, 1998, Osama called for a holy war against the United States. He included three reasons:

1. The U.S. presence in Saudi Arabia during the Gulf War
2. The U.S. involvement to prevent a Palestinian build up
3. The U.S. support of Israel

Here is the actual text:

> [1] The United States has been occupying the lands of Islam in the holiest of places, the Arabian Peninsula, plundering its riches, dictating to its rulers, humiliating its people, terrorizing its neighbors, and turning its bases in the Peninsula into a spearhead through which to fight neighboring Muslim peoples . . . [2] despite the great devastation inflicted on the Iraqi people by the crusader-Zionist alliance [US and Israel], and despite the huge number of those killed, which has exceeded 1 million . . . the Americans are once again trying to repeat the horrific massacres, as though they are not content with the protracted blockade imposed after the ferocious war or the fragmentation and devastation . . . [3] if the Americans' aims behind these wars are religious and economic, the aim is also to serve the Jew's petty state and divert attention from its occupation of Jerusalem and murder of Muslims there.[14]

He concludes that Muslims are under attack: "All these crimes and sins committed by the Americans are a clear declaration of war on God, his messenger [Muhammad], and Muslims."

The aggressive part of the message includes quotations from the Koran:

> The ruling to kill the Americans and their allies—civilians and military—is an individual duty of every Muslim who can do it in any country in which it is possible to do it, in order to liberate the al-Aqsa Mosque and the holy mosque [Mecca] from their grip, and in order for their armies to move out of all the

> lands of Islam, defeated and unable to threaten any Muslim. This is in accordance with the words of Almighty God, "and fight the pagans all together as they fight you all together," and "fight them until there is no more tumult or oppression, and there prevail justice and faith in God" . . .
>
> We with God's help—call on every Muslim who believes in God and wishes to be rewarded to comply with God's order to kill the Americans and plunder their money wherever and whenever they find it. We also call on Muslim ulema [teachers of Islamic law], leaders, youths, and soldiers to launch the raid on Satan's U.S. troops and the devil's supporters allying with them, and to displace those who are behind them so that they may learn a lesson.
>
> Almighty God said: "O ye who believe, give your response to God and His Apostle, when He calleth you to that which will give you life. And know that God cometh between a man and his heart, and that it is He to whom ye shall all be gathered."
>
> Almighty God also says: "O ye who believe, what is the matter with you, that when ye are asked to go forth in the cause of God, ye cling so heavily to the earth! Do ye prefer the life of this world to the hereafter? But little is the comfort of this life, as compared with the hereafter. Unless ye go forth, He will punish you with a grievous penalty, and put others in your place; but Him ye would not harm in the least. For God hath power over all things."[15]

Osama bin Laden called on every Muslim, in the name of Allah and what is stated in the Koran, to kill Americans and plunder their money. Unless Muslims act according to this order, Allah will punish them with a "grievous penalty." This is fundamentalism in action.

CHAPTER 3

WHY DO THEY HATE THE WEST?

Setting: Saudi Arabia, 1978, three years after the assassination of King Faisal.

The aging Muhammad bin Laden looked out the window. The Saudi landscape quivered in the afternoon heat. "Yes, I laundered some money for house of al-Saud. Is that what you want to hear? It was a small favor for all the business they had given me. Don't forget, our riches in the building industry come straight from their vast oil resources."

An idealistic youth, Osama was still concerned. He looked at the clock and wondered how long they would have privacy in a household with several wives and dozens of children. "Father, don't you think King Faisal's assassination was Allah's judgment against his involvement with the West?"

Muhammad did not, and sternly rebuked the idea. Still, Osama continued. "Many people feel that the outbreak of the Lebanese Civil War was punishment from Allah for their sins and destructive influence on young Muslims."

Muhammad gazed at his son. "It was just a few short years ago when you were one of those rich, Saudi youth flying continually to

Beirut and hanging out in the nightclubs, bars, and casinos. How many times were you out fighting, drinking, and womanizing? I told you not to, but you wouldn't listen. Beirut was bad, and it may have fallen under Allah's judgment. But the assassination of King Faisal by his deranged nephew had nothing to do with that. The king was a progressive thinker who had the interests of the country well in hand. . . . What have they been teaching you at that school?"

Osama did not answer the question but redirected his approach. "Father, I know that you were affected by the way of Islam when you rebuilt and refurbished those two holy mosques. Your change affected me, as well. I learned new things from our Islamic books, which is part of the reason I attended the university. Those professors wanted to bring Islam to a new level."

Picking up a book, he continued, "When I read Wail Uthman's *The Party of God in Struggle with the Party of Satan*, I finally understood that the real enemies of Islam are within—those who only pretend but do not live it. Anwar Sadat is such an enemy, and so are all who oppose our laws that come from the holy Koran and Hadith. Western countries pollute us with thoughts that are wrong. The streets of Jidda are full of our youth who have been influenced by their drugs and promiscuity. The United States plays both sides, supporting Israel while courting us for better oil prices. Then the oil money causes a greater divide between the have and have-nots. The whole thing stinks."

Muhammad's patience was thin. "Seek maturity! It is much harder to work for wealth than it is to simply inherit it. You could become a great man by following in my footsteps. Allah wants me to prosper so that I can help the poor and influence the world for his glory. The West needs to change, but they also have some things to offer us."

"—like trading." It was Osama's turn to stare out the window. "I cannot put my energies toward building that business. The world needs Islam. Allah gave us oil so we could fund those necessary changes. The West will come to understand that its decadence and pride will be its ruin."

While flying from the East Coast to the West Coast, I sat next to an older woman from India. She had a beauty mark on her forehead and wore traditional Indian clothing. The vast majority of the Indian population is Hindu. I easily assumed she was the same and struck up a conversation to broaden my understanding of her beliefs and, hopefully, to open her eyes to Jesus.

"Are you from India?"

"Yes, but this is not my first trip to the States. . . ." She continued with her story, telling me how her son and daughter had been educated at one of America's best universities. Now, each was married and enjoying a successful profession in a different part of the country.

The conversation was going nicely, so I ventured the question. "Are you Hindu?"

"Why no, not at all! I was raised a Christian and went to Catholic school as a child."

Now *my* eyes were open, and I was reminded that nationality and ethnic origins do not equal religious affiliation.

Similarly, immediately following the September 11 attack, authorities found a long list of clues that indicated Muslims from the Middle East were responsible. As a result, Arabs were painted with the broad brush of terrorism. Although it appears that the terrorists turned out to be Muslims from the Middle East, it does not mean that all nationalities of Middle Eastern origin deserve the moniker. There are many flag-waving Muslim-American patriots who have died defending this country. It would be a mistake to bind all Muslims and Arabs as a people bent on the destruction of the United States.

So, in order to find out *why* they hate us, we need to know exactly who *they* are? Simply put, the group that has declared war on the West is specifically the Islamic fundamentalists. With that, let's refocus the question to, "How do fundamentalist Islamic groups justify terrorism against the United States?"

There are four popular reasons:

1. The presence of U.S. troops on the "holy" ground of Saudi Arabia.
2. The U.S. and Israel alliance.
3. Western moral decline.
4. Emergence of the Islamic State.

U.S. Troops in Saudi Arabia

The U.S. involvement in the early 1990s in the Gulf War gave a major reason to Osama bin Laden and other militant Islamists to hate us. Prior to that time, Osama had been in Afghanistan developing the al-Qaeda as a part of the Afghan Mujahideen. This fighting force was battling with the Soviet Union and even backed by billions of U.S. and Saudi dollars. [1] But in 1989, bin Laden became disillusioned with the internal bickering of the Mujahideen in Afghanistan and returned home to Saudi Arabia. He was given a hero's welcome with widespread celebrity status for his decade of fighting the jihad. He tried reentering civilian life by getting involved with his family's construction business, which received numerous government contracts from Saudi royals.[2]

In 1990, Iraq invaded Kuwait. If Saddam Hussein had been successful, he would have controlled one-fifth of the world's oil reserves.[3] Osama bin Laden immediately went to Riyadh and lobbied King Fahd to raise up a Saudi army and fight against Iraq without involving the United States. It was one thing to use U.S. dollars to support the fight against the Soviet Union in Afghanistan, but it was quite another to have the infidels defiling the sacred Muslim land of Saudi Arabia.

Osama was one voice in many who wanted to keep the West away from Arabia and its holy Muslim shrines. The senior Saudi Islamic scholars (*ulema*) also were against the notion of involving America. Islamist leaders like Sheik Tamimi tried to rally support for Iraq in order to defeat the U.S. He claimed losing Kuwait was less of a priority than the threat America would bring.[4]

Osama asked the Saudi ulema to issue religious rulings (*fatwas*) against non-Muslims being in Saudi Arabia. However, King Fahd feared his kingdom would fall to Iraq. He barely managed to persuade 350 ulema at Mecca to agree with temporary aid from the United States.

As soon as the 540,000 U.S. troops arrived, the cry from Islamists was that the royal house of Saudi Arabia had just abdicated its legitimate rights to be custodians of the holy shrines of Islam. Bin Laden also criticized the action but avoided specifically insulting the royal family. He was respected in his country and did not want to jeopardize that. Osama told the king that the infidels must leave as soon as the war was over, a compromise that was growing in popularity. The Saudi royals began seeing bin Laden as a threat to their power and warned him that, if he should continue, he may lose government contracts and personal property. Even his extended family was threatened. At the same time, the Saudi intelligence community courted him in order to keep him from crossing over to anti-Saudi Islamic extremists.

However, after Kuwait's liberation in 1991, some 20,000 U.S. troops stayed on in Saudi Arabia at the king's request. Bin Laden was angry, and he left the country for Sudan in 1992. In 1994, he openly criticized the Saudi royal family and, as a result, lost his citizenship.[5] Shortly after, he made his way back to Afghanistan and befriended the leaders of the emerging Taliban movement.

Although the U.S. presence in Saudi Arabia was at the king's request, the cultural troubles between America and Arabia were evident. The American media portrayed Arabians as resentful of the U.S. occupancy and intolerant toward social change. For instance, the U.S. Christian chaplains in the armed forces were not allowed to wear crosses in their lapels. Christian services were not permitted. Soldiers were advised to leave Bibles at home because the ulema did not want a Christian presence in their country.

A source of embarrassment to the Saudis was the public demonstration by forty-seven educated, Saudi women who felt oppressed under Islamic law. Many were university professors or medical doctors. In order to capture worldwide publicity for the Saudi ban on female drivers, these women ditched their chauffeurs and drove themselves in a convoy. The reaction to their civil disobedience was immediate and loud from all Arabic sectors. The women were forbidden to speak with journalists, stage other demonstrations, or leave the country. They were even threatened with death. In the mosques, they were labeled as "red Communists, dirty American secularists, whores and prostitutes, fallen women and advocators of vice."[6] The event underscored a resentment that was growing in the Saudi community toward U.S. occupancy and cultural influence.

Islamic fundamentalists were also resentful of American actions and attitudes. When the bombs began flying against neighboring countries, there was a fear that nearby relatives could be at risk. Why was the prideful foreigner, America, interfering in disputes between Islamic "brother" nations that had worked through their own problems before? After arriving with military muscle to win a war against the Iraqi dictator-tyrant and to free the victimized Kuwait, America was seen as a prideful bully with an oil agenda. Although American troops were seen praying for God's favor, the act was insignificant to the Muslims. No matter how simple it seemed to the Americans, the locals weren't thrilled that the *Yanks* had come over with money, weapons, and technology to make everything right.

The U.S and Israel Alliance

Islam automatically resents any assistance to the Jews. So why does the U.S. continue its alliance with Israel? First, we give them political, economic, and military aid because they are the only democratic government in a region that is otherwise full of religious dictatorships. In comparison, there are over fifty Islamic countries in the world and not one of them is a democracy.[7] Additional frustration has been based on the perceived religious encouragement of the U.S. for the Jews. Some Muslims assume America's Christian heritage causes greater sympathy for the plight of Israel.

When the state of Israel emerged on May 14, 1948, it was immediately thrust into a war of independence against the neighboring Muslim nations. The U.S. has been supportive of Israel's sovereignty as a nation since its inception. Although policymakers have not always seen eye to eye, there has been enough agreement that America has been called "Israel's closest friend." On that same day, President Truman granted recognition of their provisional government. Formal recognition was granted in January 1949, and Israeli ambassadors started arriving in the United States.

Although the United States has long sought peace in the Middle East, it normally ends up either aiding Israel in its wars or recognizing Israel's right to defend itself against aggression. In October 1956, Israel used military force to quickly dispatch Egyptian, Jordanian, and Syrian soldiers who pressed in on its borders. President Eisenhower supported Israel's right to respond to intense provocation.

In 1962, President Kennedy sold Israel HAWK antiaircraft missiles. Shortly afterward, President Johnson sold them tanks and Phantom jets, which gave Israel an edge over its neighbors. These weapons helped to assure victory in the Six Day War of 1967, when Israel took control of the West Bank and the Gaza Strip and occupied the old city of Jerusalem—regained after almost two thousand years.[8] In 1996, the Jews celebrated the 3000th anniversary of Jerusalem as the ancient capitol the Jewish state; and in 1998, the 50th anniversary (the Jubilee) of the reestablishment of Israel.[9] Arab nations have not forgotten that America's weapons aided Israel in taking the city that is holy to Muslims as well.

Under the Carter and Reagan administrations, American alliance with Israel grew. To date, Israel has received close to $100 billion in aid. On top of that, Israel enjoys links to U.S. missile warning satellite systems and hotlines between the Pentagon and the Israeli Defense Ministry, plus strategic cooperation in our intelligence communities. This kind of alliance provided an open channel for the Israeli secret intelligence (Mossad) to inform the FBI and CIA in August 2001 that some 200 terrorists were slipping across American borders for "a major assault on the United States." Israel cautioned that it had picked up indications of a large-scale target in the United States and that Americans would be "very vulnerable".[10] Interestingly, other Islamic nations who have been friendly to the United States—such as Jordan, Egypt, and Saudi Arabia—did not offer any intelligence.

The four largest Muslim nations are Indonesia, Pakistan, Bangladesh, and India—none of which are part of the Middle East.

Examining the historical religious issues of Arab resentment toward the U.S.-Israel alliance, it becomes evident that political support of Israel is viewed as favoritism for the Jewish faith and *against* Islam.

The struggle over religious ownership of Israel, especially Jerusalem, predates America's involvement by thousands of years. Jews, Christians, and Muslims have each occupied Jerusalem—even multiple times—in their histories. All three of these monotheistic religions trace their natural or spiritual heritage roots back to Abraham, who lived in the area of Jerusalem.

For Muslims, the Dome of the Rock in Jerusalem is holy. It was built by Caliph 'Abd al-Malik between AD 689 and 691 on what is considered by both Muslims and Jews to be ancient Mt. Moriah. Muslims believe it to be the miraculous place from which Muhammad, accompanied by the angel Gabriel, stepped to take his visionary ascension into heaven.[11] That night, he supposedly visited the seven heavens and spoke with Adam, Idris, Moses, Jesus, and Abraham.[12]

For the Jews, tradition says that this rock is none other than the symbolic foundation upon which the world was created. It is also believed that this is the same rock upon which Abraham bound Isaac (see Genesis 22:9) in preparation for sacrifice, and it is believed to be the location of the Solomon's temple.

For Christians, Jerusalem is honored to some degree for the Jewish traditions. More importantly, it is honored as the city where the Lord Jesus was crucified and rose from the dead three days later. The foundations of both the Hebrew and Christian faiths are woven into Jerusalem's history up to the Roman siege in AD 70.[13]

Islamic fundamentalists perceive America as a Judeo-Christian culture hostile toward a Muslim occupation of Jerusalem. It is a common understanding that the United States was greatly influenced by Christianity when it was founded. Some Islamic groups assume all Americans are Christians. Consequently, they want all Americans to suffer for allowing what they perceive to be Christianity's modern crusade against Islam to continue.

Incidents in the last couple of years confirm Jewish and Christian fears that Palestinian Muslims are out to destroy their religious sites. Muslims have made attempts to take over Joseph's tomb and Rachel's tomb; build a mosque in Bethlehem's Manger Square, including a minaret that towers above the Church of the Nativity's bell tower; and have begun construction on a mosque in Jerusalem at the Golden Gate, which is destroying ancient Israeli artifacts. The Palestinian National Authority has dubbed the current move of Islam to overtake Jewish and Christian sites as the "Intifada of Al-Aqsa".[14] These events have made Israel wonder if any of the Hebrew and Christian holy sites would actually be preserved safely in an Islamic society.

Western Moral Decline

My wife and I have European friends who fear traveling to the United States because of the violence that has erupted on school campuses and in public places over the past decades. One friend had visited America as a teenager in the early 1970s. She loved it. Now, she is too concerned about her welfare to return. From a small, peaceful community in northern Idaho, my wife and I have a hard time relating to her concerns. We see a far more peaceful America than is represented worldwide in media headlines.

Islamic fundamentalists see those headlines. They do not appreciate the social advances we have made regarding the freedom of religion, civil rights, and the equality of women. They do not value our breakthroughs in science and medicine, nor the humanitarian aid that is poured out to other countries. Our technological achievements are counted against us as pride and Western economic intimidation. America is perceived as Christianity's child. Since Islam is perceived as superior and more accurate, Christian assistance is regarded as a danger to the moral fabric of Islamic society. When we export our goods, we also export our culture, which undermines the Islamic way of life.

After reviewing a sample of prime-time broadcasts from Hollywood, it's easy to understand how America could be seen to be insincere and unethical as a "Christian nation." Violence has grown in the United States, as have pornography, gambling, theft, murder, occultism, cults, American-bred terrorists, and many other amoral types of behavior. Abortion and euthanasia have been legalized. Gay rights and fortune telling are encouraged. The U.S. entertainment industry has a growing interest in Gothic and satanic topics. Suicide, murder, and vile behavior are promoted as amusement or protected under the rights of free expression. Until the attack on America, God had been banned from almost every public arena—except for the text "In God We Trust" inscribed on the currency.

In countries where freedom of thought is allowed, there will always be new movements in the arts, in literature, science, religion, and politics that may transfer the moral standard from a religious to a secular base. But such transitions may not add to the longevity or richness of the culture.

Emergence of the Islamic State

When Hasan al-Banna created the Muslim Brotherhood in Egypt in1928, he taught principles and doctrines that are still fueling the fundamentalist movement today. One of these is the concept of the Islamic state. The proposed state is similar to the one set up by the prophet Muhammad in the seventh-century city of Medina. The Islamic law (*Shariah*) based on the Koran and Hadith governs the entire political, economic, and social system, including proper greeting, suitable clothing, education, jurisdiction, the equality of believers, and the proper roles of women.

The proposed Islamic state was at the heart of the 1979 bloody revolution of Iran, where the Islamic preacher, Ayatollah Khomeini, ousted the pro-Western monarchy of Shaw Muhammad Reza Pahlevi. Khomeini was originally exiled from Iran in 1964 for aggressive demonstrations against the Shaw and Western culture. Once in power, Khomeini replaced Iran's Western European legal system with a strict religious government. John Esposito, an author and expert on Islam, wrote: "Export of revolutionary Islam sprang from the Ayatollah Khomeini's ideological worldview, an interpretation of Islam which combined a religiously rooted brand of Iranian nationalism with a belief in the transnational character and global mission of Muslims to spread Islam through preaching and example as well as armed struggle."[15]

Similar notions drive the majority of modern Islamic struggles. In their thinking, the best societies are based on Islamic law. Tolerance for other religions, such as Christianity and Judaism, is available if members of those faiths fully support Islamic law and give financially.

Even though the various factions of Islamic fundamentalists might not agree on everything, "They share a tendency to consider their opinions the only valid ones, and are united in their disapproval of the supposedly 'amoral' life of the West. They repudiate interest in any kind of dialogue, and they strictly reject a division between religion and state."[16]

The American system of separating church and state is, to them, something Allah did not plan. Thus, their worldview often fails to distinguish between U.S. government policies and U.S. religious institutions. In 1964, this worldview gave rise to the Palestinian Liberation Organization (PLO) under the leadership of Yassir Arafat, a devout Muslim. Ever since, Arafat has been working to free Israel from the Jews, despite aid from the United States.[17]

Most Islamic fundamentalist groups pose problems for:

1. The United States and the West
2. The traditional Islamic teachers who are caught between the terrorists and modernization
3. The American Muslim population that wants to express the best of its religious traditions rather than the worst

Indeed, it must be remembered, "About half the Muslims in the West today have been born there to parents who immigrated in the 1950s and 1960s."[18] These 3 million people may be appalled at what Islamic fundamentalists are doing. And they also may be questioning the roots of their faith, asking themselves what is it in their religious history that has produced the "fruit of jihad."

In his book, *Taliban: Militant Islam, Oil, & Fundamentalism in Central Asia*, the Pakistani journalist and author Ahmed Rashid wrote: "Many Western commentators do not particularize the Taliban, but condemn Islam wholesale for being intolerant and antimodern. The Taliban, like so many Islamic fundamentalist groups, today, divest Islam of all its legacies except theology—Islamic philosophy, science, arts, aesthetics and mysticism are ignored. Thus the rich diversity of Islam and the essential message of the Koran—to build a civil society that is just and equitable in which rulers are responsible for their citizens—is forgotten"[19]

Is it truly the goal of the Koran, and thus Islam, to build a civil society that is just and equitable?

PART TWO

THE HISTORICAL ROOTS OF ISLAM

——— ✡ ✝ ☪ ———

CHAPTER 4

IT ALL STARTED WITH ABRAHAM

Setting: Evening on a hillside in Arabia at the end of the sixth century.

Abd hugged his grandson with one arm and with the hand of the other pointed toward the bright orb in the sky. "There," he exclaimed, "Do you see it, Muhammad?"

The six-year-old cocked his head. "Yes, I see it. Tell me the story again."

Abd heard the other men chuckle. He answered softly, "Well, there are so many stories about Allah and about the heavens. Which one do you want to hear?"

"Tell me about the face and what happened when I was born." Abd took a deep breath and faithfully related the story of how Allah revealed himself through his face on the moon so that people would realize that he was the greatest of the gods in the heavens. The sun goddess, Allah's wife, and the other gods were also powerful, but nothing like Allah. He was supreme.

"What about when I was born?" said Muhammad.

"All right, but then it's time to sleep." Abd stared at the rising moon. "When you were born, I gave praise to Allah. Allah was hiding much of himself that night but let me see just enough so that I think maybe one of his eye's winked at me. There were bright stars out that night, and I had a dream that you would be like a bright light. Of course, it was also during the year when Abraha's army and a large elephant came to destroy the Kabah. But Allah caused the birds of the air to carry stones and drop them on the elephant and Abraha's whole army. They were wounded and got diseases in their sores. So they fled and left us alone."

The little boy looked up. "Was that to protect me, Grandfather?"

"I can't really say, but I do know that you are very special to Allah. Now, off to bed with you."

As Muhammad headed for the tent, his grandfather mourned silently the lost Abdullah, the boy's father. Turning to the other men, Abd said, "He is a good boy."

Quss ibn Saida spoke up, "Yes, but is it wise to make him feel so special, telling him rumors and myths? You know there are bright stars every night."

"You worry about your own family. Muhammad still hurts from the death of both parents. It is good to tell him he is special. Besides, some of what I told him is true."

Hulais Ibn Alkama, the Bedouin, joined in, "Are you defending the moon face to us again? Come on, Abd. It is obviously fate and Al-Manat that control everything?" Smatterings of comments throughout the group defended Al-Lat as the highest goddess or Al-Uzza as the most powerful. Everyone had his favorite.

Quss spoke above the rest. "It is none of those. It is Al-Rahman, the Merciful. He is the most powerful."

Abd turned and faced Quss. "Well, for one who supposedly serves a merciful god, you sure don't seem to possess any." The remark hung in the silence.

Waraka, another in the group, said, "As for me, I am now more and more inclined to agree with the Hanifs. There is only one god and he is the god of Abraham."

No one noticed the small figure that had just emerged until Abd said, "Muhammad, why are you back?"

"I heard the loud voices and was afraid."

Abd grabbed the boy in his arms. "I will come with you this time." Then, looking around at the group, he continued, "Muhammad, these are good men. But always remember that if there is only one god, it must be Allah. Who else could create such a beautiful peaceful light and a face to watch over us at night?" Muhammad smiled at the comforting thought.

Abraham, the patriarch, is an important figure in the religious history of Christians, Jews, and Muslims. Interestingly, the Koran states that Abraham was a Muslim. "Abraham was neither Jew nor Christian; but he was sound in faith, a Muslim" (Sura 3:60)[1] A better understanding of why Abraham's ancestral connection is important to Islam can be gained from a review of his life as recorded in the Bible.

We first read about Abram (later to be called Abraham) in Genesis. God called him to leave his country and family and move to a new land. There, God would bless him, make him a great nation, bless those who blessed him, and curse those who cursed him, and in Abram "all the families of the earth shall be blessed" (Gen. 12:3).

Arriving in Canaan, God promised him, "To your descendents I will give this land" (12:7). However, Abram confessed his fear to the Lord, saying one of his servants would have to be the heir because he had no son. The Lord responded: "This one shall not be your heir, but one who will come from your own body shall be your heir" (15:5). Abraham was seventy-five years old, but he was learning that God's plans are not fulfilled through man's efforts. They are fulfilled through His grace and in His time.

Time passed and there was still no son. His wife, Sarai, was barren. So she told Abram to take her servant, Hagar, and conceive a son through her. Hagar conceived a son when Abram was 86.

The pregnancy caused great difficulties between the two women. Finally, Hagar fled from Sarai's jealousy and escaped to the wilderness. God heard her cries and told her to return to Sarai and submit to her authority. He also said the name of Hagar's son should be *Ishmael*, meaning "God will hear." God assured Hagar that Ishmael's descendants would be tremendous—too many to count. In addition came a prophecy regarding Ishmael's character:

> Behold, you are with child,
> And you shall bear a son.
> You shall call his name Ishmael,
> Because the Lord had heard your
> Affliction.
> He shall be a wild man,
> His hand shall be against every man,
> And every man's hand against him.
> And he shall dwell in the presence of
> All his brethren. (Gen. 16:11–12)

Hagar returned and submitted to Sarai and Abram.

God still had his plan. To prepare Abram and Sarai's hearts for their own son, as He promised, God changed their names.

> Then God said to Abraham, "As for Sarai your wife, you shall not call her name Sarai, but Sarah shall be her name. And I will bless her and also give you a son by her; then I will bless her, and

> she shall be a mother of nations; kings of peoples shall be from her."
>
> Then Abraham fell on his face and laughed, and said in his heart, "Shall a child be born to a man who is one hundred years old? And shall Sarah, who is ninety years old, bear a child? And Abraham said to God, "Oh, that Ishmael might live before You!"
>
> Then God said: "No, Sarah your wife shall bear a son, and you shall call his name Isaac; I will establish my covenant with him for an everlasting covenant, and with his descendents after him.
>
> "And as for Ishmael, I have heard you. Behold, I have blessed him, and will make him fruitful, and will multiply him exceedingly. He shall beget twelve princes, and I will make him a great nation.
>
> "But My covenant I will establish with Isaac, whom Sarah shall bear to you at this set time next year." (Gen. 17:15–21)

The word Isaac means *laughter,* and it appears that the Lord chose that name in response to Abraham's laughter. When Sarah heard the plan for them to have a child in their old age, she laughed too. Yet, soon their laughter turned into shouts of joy when the son they were promised was born (Gen. 18:12–15; 21:6).

Ishmael

> He shall be a wild man,
> His hand shall be against every man,
> And every man's hand against him.
> And he shall dwell in the presence of
> All his brethren. (Gen. 16:12)

The Hebrew words used in the passage for "wild man" are *pere' adam*. *Adam*, in Hebrew, is translated as "man;" and *pere'* gives the sense of running wild. Out of the ten times it is used in the Old Testament, nine times refers specifically to the trait of a stubborn, independent, or untamed ass.[2] The only other reference is used to describe Ishmael. This prophecy refers not only to Ishmael but also to his sons and to their descendants, namely, the Ishmaelites, who were nomadic Bedouins and wandering Arabs.[3]

In fulfillment of the prophecy, Ishmael had the spirit of a wild man and feuded throughout his life. As Isaac and Ishmael grew up together, contention often broke out. Sarah asked Abraham to send Hagar and Ishmael away, and Abraham did so. Because Ishmael was also a son, the Lord assured Abraham the boy would become a great nation (Gen. 21:8–21). As that nation grew, Ishmael fought for the causes of his brethren across the Arabian Peninsula. Then Ishmael transferred that spirit into his twelve sons, the princes of the Arabic nations.

In Genesis 25:13–15 we are told that Ishmael's twelve sons lived to the east of the Hebrews. The Ishmaelites were nomadic tribes that wandered throughout northern Arabia. The Jewish historian Josephus described them as "an Arabian nation."[4] Today, many Muslims claim Ishmael as their direct ancestor and that all of Arabia descended from him. Others, more accurately, claim that many people groups came together to comprise Arabia. Biblical evidence reveals Abraham had other offspring after Sarah's death. His wife Keturah gave him many children. Before his death, Abraham gave gifts to each of his heirs and sent them east to the Arabian Peninsula, away from his son Isaac (Gen. 25:6).

Local tradition has it that Hagar and Ishmael originally settled in Mecca. Abraham visited them there and helped Ishmael rebuild the Kabah, a cube-style building that had originally been erected by Adam but had fallen into disrepair.[5] The Kabah was the local temple, a very important site of worship for the community and for pilgrims who journeyed there.

The World and Early Life of Muhammad

Almost 2600 years after the time of Abraham and Ishmael, Muhammad, the founder of Islam, was born in Mecca on the Arabian Peninsula. During his life, he exhibited similar characteristics to those of Ishmael.

Muhammad was born in AD 570 to Abdullah (Abd-Allah) and Aminah. Tradition indicates that on the night of his birth, a star illuminated the heavens and that his umbilical cord was severed by providence with human aid. As a child, two angels supposedly visited him. They opened his breast with their bare hands and washed his heart with snow until it was as pure as a crystal.[6]

The vast Arabian Peninsula was in a lull from warfare that had raged for decades between two great empires to the north. The Zoroastrian Persian Empire stretched from Iraq to Afghanistan, and the Christian Byzantine Empire was composed of Asia Minor, Syria, Egypt, Abyssinia, and southeast Europe.[7] The religious and political struggles over the peninsula had exhausted the people and drained the resources of these empires. For the time being, peace reigned. Viorst says, "In time the wars in Arabia would resume, but the attackers would be Muhammad's followers, seeking to establish their new faith, before turning their attention to Byzantine and Persian conquerors."[8]

In the days of Muhammad's childhood, while the two empires were not fighting over the peninsula, there were many skirmishes between the tribes of Arabia. Survival demanded loyalty, discipline, and vigilance.[9] Some historians think there was a population explosion in the Bedouin community that stressed the limited water and food resources. This group then became more urbanized. Muhammad was born into the Quraysh tribe, the preeminent traders of Mecca. His father was a part of the Hashim clan of Quraysh tribe. However, before

Non-Arab Muslims out number Arab Muslims three to one.

Muhammad was born, his father died; and his mother passed away when he was only six.[10] Historical accounts claim that Muhammad's mother practiced occultism, had visions, and claimed that spirits or jinns visited her.[11]

After her death, Muhammad lived with his grandfather, the guardian of the Kabah temple.[12] A strong bond of love formed between them. Unfortunately, after only two years, Muhammad's grandfather died. The boy was passed around to relatives and eventually landed in the custody of his poor uncle Abu Talib. Muhammad became accustomed to living simply and began to work at an early age. There is disagreement over whether Muhammad received any education as a child. He did, however, receive training in weapons of war.[13]

At this time, Mecca was a thriving, important center for trade caravans. It was described as a place where "no waters flow . . . not a blade of grass on which to rest the eye . . . only merchants there."[14]

The Religious Culture

At the time of Muhammad, the religious system was varied. Several monotheistic cults had been established in southern Arabia, including one to al-Rahman "the merciful." Later, that name was to find prominence in the Koran as one of the most favorite descriptions of Allah.[15] There was a group known as the Hanifs (Arabic for "the upright"), who said they were the spiritual descendents of Abraham and ascribed to the worship of a single, highly personal deity. The Bedouins basically believed that fate ruled their destiny.

Throughout the Arabian Peninsula, there was a vast amount of idolatry. Many gods and idols were worshipped, and there was a great restlessness in Mecca as a result. The Arabs knew that the religions of Judaism and Christianity had a longer history, thus were more sophisticated than their own beliefs and rituals. As a result, some of the Quraysh tribe had come to believe that the high god of their pantheon, Allah (al-*Lah*), was the same deity worshipped by the Jews and Christians.[16]

The worship of Allah might have preceded Muhammad and the Koran by over a thousand years. Some scholars believe the word *Allah*, which means "the god," was derived from the ancient Aramaic word *elahh*. This term can be found in the Bible (i.e., Daniel 6:23 and Ezra 4:24). If the connection is correct, the name likely was altered in Muhammad's time and associated with a moon deity, the head of their pantheon.

As was the case in many ancient cultures, there was a pantheon of deities headed by one god. Leading pantheons from other cultures included

- Egyptians: Atum
- Greeks: Zeus
- Romans: Jupiter
- Phoenicians: Baal
- Ugarit: El
- Assyrian: Assur
- Babylonian: Ea
- Sumer: Enlil

There were also numerous deities that were male and female couples, such as Baal and Astarte; El and Athirat; or Zeus and Hera. Most ancient regions, cities, and tribes had their own patron deity that presided over the others. This system of idol worship had been around for eons.[17]

Most early cultures, including most of the Ancient Near East, worshipped the moon as a female deity and the sun as a male deity. However, it was the reverse among the Arabs. Muhammad's tribe, the Quraysh, was particularly devoted to Allah, the moon diety, and his daughters. Author Robert Morey, a Christian apologist who has conducted extensive research on Islam, makes an interesting observation:

> In Arabia, the sun god was viewed as a female goddess and the moon as the male god. As has been pointed out by many scholars such as Alfred Guilluame, the moon god was called by

various names, one of which was Allah! The name of Allah was used as a personal name of the moon god, in addition to other titles that could be given to him.

Allah, the moon god, was married to the sun goddess. Together they produced three goddesses who were called "the daughters of Allah." These three goddesses were called Al-Lat, Al-Uzza, and Manat.[18]

Muhammad and the Koran

Muhammad grew up and worked as a camel driver until age 25. At this time he married Khadijah, a rich widow. Some historians say she was 15 years older than Muhammad. Others dispute this because she bore him seven children, which would be unlikely for a woman already forty. Khadijah owned a fruit business in Mecca. Muhammad assumed responsibilities for it and ran the business for fifteen years. Marriage brought to Muhammad wealth and social position. Of the six or seven children they had, the boys died in infancy, but four daughters survived into adulthood. From what we know of their marriage, Muhammad and Khadijah had a happy, monogamous relationship for two decades until her death.[19]

Tradition has it that in AD 610, on the seventeenth day of Ramadan, Muhammad went to pray in a cave on Mount Hira. It was here that Gabriel the angel first acted as an intermediary speaking the word of God (see Sura 96). Muhammad told people that these were the direct words from Allah, the one supreme god whom they should all worship.

Based on a culture of oral traditions, the revelations were not written down at first. Muhammad eventually had scribes write down the words, but the collection was not completely assembled until after his death. This collection of revelations became known as the Koran.

Islam holds that the Koran is a verbatim record of God's speech. In Arabic, the word *Koran* means "recitation," implying that the text is an exact recitation of Allah's words to Muhammad. In order to be a Muslim one must believe in God's absolute authorship. Thus, believers maintain that the Koran is a perfect book.

When Muhammad started preaching, his probable intention was to rid his tribe from idolatry. Only later did he expand his vision and purposely embark on the creation of a whole new religion. A convert to Muhammad's religion would eventually be called a *Muslim*, meaning "one who is submitted to God."

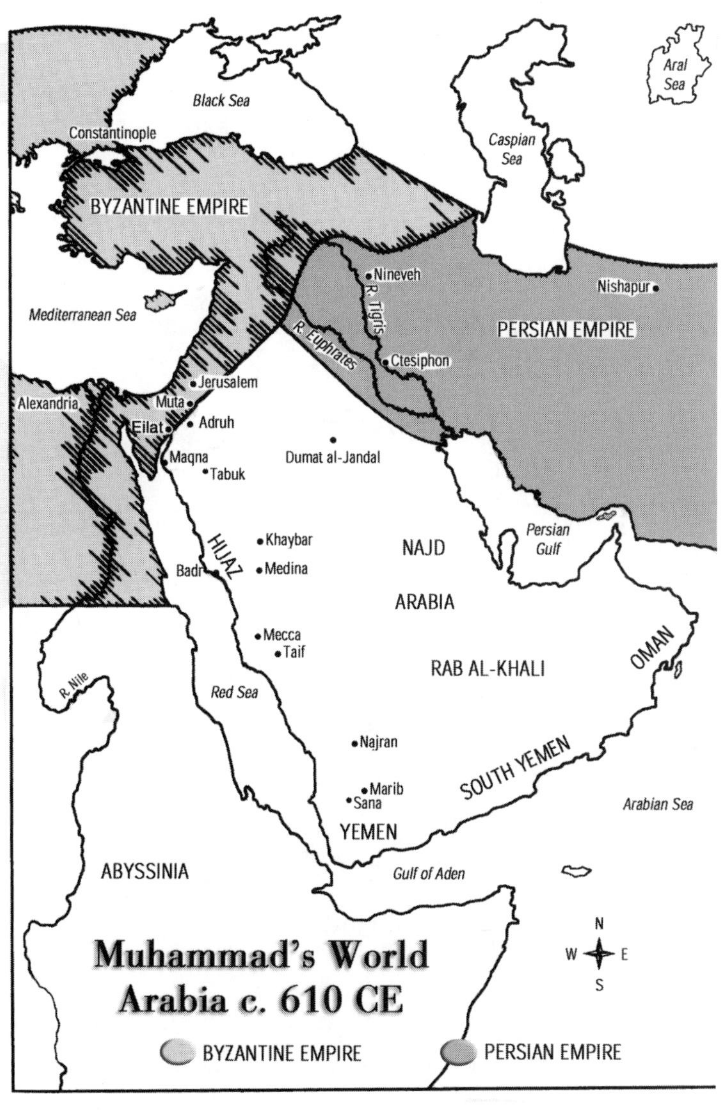

Timeline: The Rise of Islam

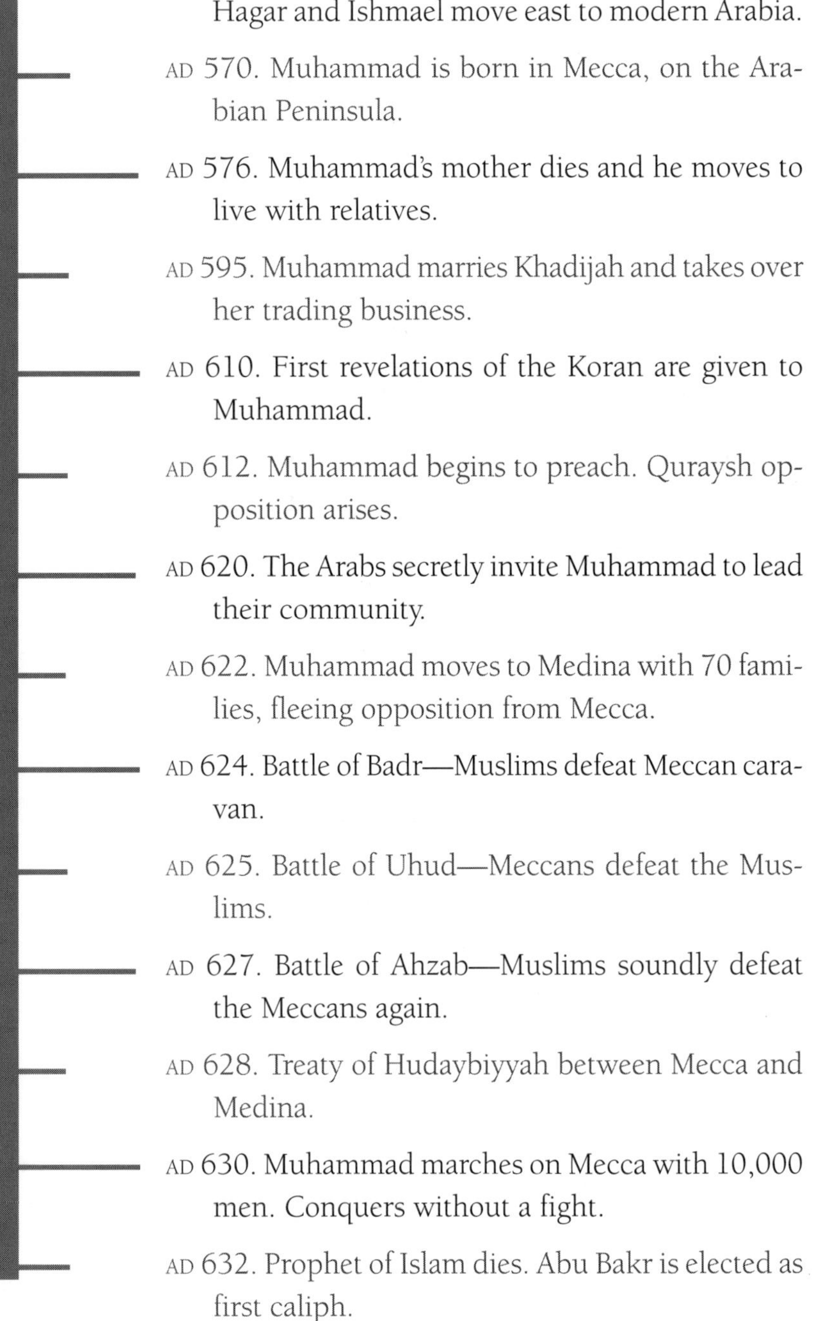

2000 BC. Abraham and Hagar have a son, Ishmael. Hagar and Ishmael move east to modern Arabia.

AD 570. Muhammad is born in Mecca, on the Arabian Peninsula.

AD 576. Muhammad's mother dies and he moves to live with relatives.

AD 595. Muhammad marries Khadijah and takes over her trading business.

AD 610. First revelations of the Koran are given to Muhammad.

AD 612. Muhammad begins to preach. Quraysh opposition arises.

AD 620. The Arabs secretly invite Muhammad to lead their community.

AD 622. Muhammad moves to Medina with 70 families, fleeing opposition from Mecca.

AD 624. Battle of Badr—Muslims defeat Meccan caravan.

AD 625. Battle of Uhud—Meccans defeat the Muslims.

AD 627. Battle of Ahzab—Muslims soundly defeat the Meccans again.

AD 628. Treaty of Hudaybiyyah between Mecca and Medina.

AD 630. Muhammad marches on Mecca with 10,000 men. Conquers without a fight.

AD 632. Prophet of Islam dies. Abu Bakr is elected as first caliph.

CHAPTER 5

MUHAMMAD THE PROPHET-WARRIOR

Setting: On the road from Medina to Mecca, early 7th century Arabia.

W*hat happened? Where am I? Oh, not again!* It had happened quickly while returning from a business meeting in Medina. On the way home to Mecca, suddenly *bam*—convulsions, shaking, and everything went black.

Muhammad's head swam in the darkening twilight. *How long have I been here?* His camel was still standing nearby, watching the middle-aged man try to gain his balance.

I hate this. He vaguely recalled falling off, then sheepishly looked around for other travelers who might have seen. Nobody. *Good.*

His whole life had been a series of these interruptions. Some people mocked him; others pitied him, thinking he was sick. Was he possessed by demons? Or were madmen actually holy vessels set aside for some great purpose? He could still hear his grandfather's gentle words: "Muhammad, honor Allah and he will use you."

The camel seemed ready to go as Muhammad mounted and headed off to Mecca. A full moon rose quietly in the sky. As the camel walked, methodically plodding each step and swaying for the next, thoughts of Khadijah easily took over his mind. *She'll be proud of me again for the wise business decisions, and she'll let me know it.*

But soon, the questions lengthened with the moonlit shadows. Were the strange seizures actually from the moon god, manifestations by Allah to get his attention? That would certainly bring respect. A trader had told him that some holy men are so far out on the edge that they can be mistaken for being mad. That would make sense. His grandfather was certainly holy. Muhammad felt that he also was unique, even better than those who had never suffered as he had. Perhaps he should investigate the religious traditions and stories more and compare himself to ancient holy men. Tonight, he would go to the Kabah and bow before the black stone and pray for enlightenment.

Originally, Muhammad's friends and tribe members did not accept his revelations or his claim to be an apostle of Allah. About two years after he received the first revelation, he started to preach his message. Yet, his actions were strange for one calling himself a prophet.

When Muhammad received a revelation, it was often accompanied by a seizure—possibly epileptic. At first, he feared that he might be demon possessed and even thought of taking his own life. However, he had another prophetic seizure with instructions not to commit suicide.

The seizures not only caused confusion among witnesses as to the source of Muhammad's revelations, but it has made many historical scholars wonder as well. Of course, Muslims embrace Muhammad and his message in faith, but they must allow others to interpret it for themselves. Just as Muslims are free to interpret the seizures as divine visitations, non-Muslims are free to interpret them as epileptic seizures, demon possession, an overactive imagination, fraud, or religious hysteria.[1]

Muhammad's wife, Khadijah, was the first to believe him. She encouraged him in the visions, telling him that he was a good man; therefore, the visitations must be from God and not demons. Next, his cousins Ali and Zaid and a friend named Abu Bakr joined him. His following slowly grew, but there was continuous opposition from members of the Quraysh.[2]

In order to appease idolatrous factions in the tribe, he claimed to have had a revelation that it was all right to worship the three idol daughters of Allah: Al-Lat, Al-Uzza, and Manat. The daughters of Allah were to be exalted; and they, in turn, would intercede on behalf of the people. This caused the idolaters to be more open to Muhammad's apostleship. Here is a part of Sura 53, the Sura of the star. The last three lines were later deleted.

> Did you consider al-Lat and al-Uzza
> And al-Manat, the third, the other?
> Those are the swans exalted:
> Their intercession is expected:
> Their likes are not neglected.[3]

This revelation got Muhammad in a lot of trouble. The text eventually came to be known as the "satanic verses" because either Muhammad gave into the temptation of Satan (*Shaitan*) to compromise, or Satan's influence caused Muhammad to recite something not from God. Could Satan slip in false verses without the prophet noticing it? The implications of this would be devastating for the new monotheistic religion.

Soon, some of his faithful followers convinced the prophet to reverse this view. He did so, and the verses were altered (A point of contention and debate ever since). When Muhammad recanted, the tension grew more with the chaffed factions because now he was proclaiming that absolute obedience should be given to Allah alone.

The word *Islam* means "submission." The person who submits is a Muslim.

In AD 620 the prophet was approached secretly by Arabs from the settlement of Yathrib (later called Medina) and asked to lead their community. He did not move there immediately. He continued in Mecca, along with the opposition from the Quraysh.

By AD 622, three years after his wife and uncle had died, the opposition to Muhammad was so great in Mecca that he decided to move. First, he went to Taif, but he found no converts there. Suras 46:29–35 and 72:1–28 tell us that on his way back to Mecca he preached to the jinns (genies) and converted them to Islam. These spirits in turn preached Islam to the people. This is probably fictitious, but it reveals the prophet's shamanistic tendencies.[4]

Not ready for more contention in Mecca, Muhammad soon decided to move his religious operations to Yathrib (Medina). This included a community of about seventy families. Author Robert Morey estimates the significance with this insight: "This move was of great significance in the development of Islam. Muslims use the date of the migration, the Hijra, as the start of the Muslim era [calendar] . . . The people were united into one single community, a brotherhood, called the Umma [same as Ummah]. The unity was no longer based on tribe, clan, or blood relationships but on their status as believers, united by faith in the one God and Muhammad his apostle."[5] Whereas one tribe dominated Mecca, the Quraysh, Medina was divided into two Arab tribes: the Aus and Kainuka.

Until Muhammad's move, a longstanding feud existed between the Arabs. Muhammad united the city under his leadership.

Medina also was home to three Jewish tribes and a Christian community. It is obvious that the teachings of the Jews and Christians in Medina helped to prepare the people for Muhammad's message. At the same time, the Jews and Christians probably supplied Muhammad with new information for his revelations, including the concepts of monotheism, the resurrection, and the importance of developing one authoritative document. It was also during this time in Medina that Muhammad tried to interest the Jews and Christians in his new religion. Muhammad used the term *prophet* for the Jews and *apostle* for the Christians in all of his teachings. As soon as they rejected his teachings and his claims to be prophet and apostle, enmity emerged in the relationship.

Until this time, Muhammad's proselytizing had been strange but not violent. Now, his methods changed. Obtaining his vision required more than a spirit of prophecy; it required a warrior spirit—intolerance mixed with a wild, barbaric spirit.

Rise of Muhammad

During the years that Muhammad lived in Medina, several battles with the Meccans helped establish Islam in Arabia. He first showed his militant power in the Nakha Raid, where he sent men to attack a caravan. One enemy man was killed, others were captured for ransom, and the caravan was looted.

In 624 AD, Muhammad defeated a large caravan of Meccans who were threatening Medina. It became known as the Battle of Badr. One year later, in the battle of Uhud, the Meccans attacked the Muslims. At first, it appeared the Muslims would win but then the Meccans counterattacked. The Muslims fell apart, and Muhammad was almost killed, suffering a stab wound in the mouth by a sword.

In AD 627, the Meccans joined forces with strong Jewish tribes in the area and marched to attack Medina in the Battle of Ahzab. However, the city had dug a large trench to protect itself.[6] The Muslims attacked and put them on the run. Muhammad repaid the Jewish settlements by looting and killing. “After one Jewish town had surrendered, 700 to 1,000 men were beheaded in one day while all the women and children were sold into slavery.”[7]

After the battles, a treaty was drawn between Mecca and Muhammad supposedly to protect the interests and religious beliefs of both for ten years. However, Muhammad broke the treaty and marched on Mecca.

In AD 630 during the holy month of Ramadan, Muhammad lead a great army of 10,000 men to Mecca. The residents submitted, and he entered the city peacefully. Most of the people became Muslims. The 360 idols in the Kabah were destroyed with exception of the black stone that represented Allah. Muhammad was now the undisputed leader. Arab tribesmen flocked to him, and Islam swept through Arabia. He returned to Medina and lived there until his sudden death in AD 632 at the age of 62.

Social Accomplishments

Muhammad brought to the Arabs a whole new religion and way of life by providing them with the Koran, a soon-to-be written, lasting testimony of Muhammad’s beliefs. He was ultimately successful in uniting the Arabs behind his cause. As is the case with some other religious founders, he identified a need in the population and sold them a vision with a more systematic approach to life. This new religious cult flourished in the spiritual vacuum that once existed.

Cults provide things for people who are drifting and feeling lost. They provide a sense of purpose, family, community, ownership, and direction for one’s own destiny. Of course, the problem with cults, in general, is that they tell people how to think and there are harsh penalties for bucking the system—all true with Islam. Muhammad established a way of life that envelopes each waking hour of the day with spiritual rituals.

The prophet's message curbed archaic blood feuds between tribes, established a spiritual equality among Muslims, increased moral behavior, and outlined instructions for charity and helping the poor. His message encouraged monotheism by promoting the worship of the God of Abraham—misnamed Allah—after the supreme god of their idolatrous pantheon.

Although he did not provide for social equality among women and men, Muhammad was able to advance the condition of women by improving the fairness of marriage and divorce laws. He also gave women the right to an inheritance and the right to own property.

Spiritual Problems of Character

Although Muhammad brought spiritual and social transformation to the Arabs, it cannot be denied that his methods and character reveal serious problems. After moving to Medina, the warring side of Muhammad's personality emerged and he sent out Abdallah Ibn Jahsh with eight men to raid a caravan. This became known as the Nakha Raid. It was on the last day of the month of Rajab, a month considered holy by the Arabs as a time of truce. Yet, the raid was made. In it, one victim was killed and the caravan captured.

When word got out, Muhammad was accused of breaking the truce. He denied that he gave the orders for the attack during the sacred month and repudiated the actions of his men. He also refused to take any of the booty—at first. Then he received the revelation of Sura 2:214 that denounced the attack but justified him taking the loot for "the cause of Allah." In the classic book *Mohammad: The Man and His Faith*, author Tor Andrae explains the character flaw: "What offends us is the calculating slyness with which he cleverly provokes Abdallah's action without assuming any responsibility for what occurred. This event reveals a trait of his character, which is particularly uncongenial to the ideals of manliness of the Nordic races. He lacks the courage to defend an opinion openly, revealing a certain tendency to dodge and take advantage of subterfuges, to avoid an open espousal of his position."[8]

It also reveals dishonesty, greed, and a lack of loyalty to the adherent's following his command. Muhammad was an accomplice to the entire devious plot in which he broke three of the Ten Commandments: "You shall not murder . . . You shall not steal . . . You shall not bear false witness" (Exodus 20:13,15,16).

Whenever the prophet needed to make an adjustment in the attitude of those around him, he would reveal a Sura—at times, for personal gain. In Sura 33:4, the prophet reveals Allah's command to keep people from bothering him:

> O Believers! Enter not into the houses of the Prophet, save by his leave, for a meal, without waiting his time. When ye are invited then enter, and when ye have eaten then disperse at once. And engage not in familiar talk, for this would cause the Prophet trouble, and he would be ashamed to bid you go; but God is not ashamed to say the truth. And when ye would ask any gift of his wives, ask it from behind the veil. Purer will this be for your hearts and for their hearts. And ye must not trouble the Apostle of God.

Another example of the prophet's manipulation is found in his relationship with his adopted son, Zaid, and Zaid's wife, Zainab. Muhammad was only six years older than Zaid and thought that Zainab was beautiful. He made overtures toward her that aroused her ambitions to be married to the prophet. Zaid felt inferior and could not handle Zainab's continual comparison of his lack to Muhammad's greatness. Zaid approached Muhammad and gave him permission to take Zainab as his wife. Muhammad refused because of the scandal that would result—at first. Then he received the revelation of Sura 33:37 that it was Allah's will for Zainab to be given to Muhammad. So Zainab divorced Zaid and married Muhammad.

As he rose to power, so did his harem of women. He had at least sixteen wives, two slaves, and four mistresses. One of the slaves, Mary, was a Christian and refused to marry him and so remained a slave. One of his wives was only eight or nine years old when Muhammad took her to bed. He did all of this against his own revelation from Allah that allows a man to marry no more than four women (Sura 4:3).

Every country run by Moslem theocrats is a totalitarian state.

The prophet became a warrior for his own advancement. At the battle of Uhud, he killed an enemy with his own hands. Greed was displayed in the large booty he amassed from raids on innocent towns and caravans. Those who opposed his religious views usually ended up dead. All three of the Jewish tribes he came to lead in Medina were objects of his wrath. Two of the tribes had to give him all their possessions and leave the town. In fear that the other tribe would cause him problems, he allowed a vengeful Arab to have his wish. The men were all beheaded and the women and children sold into slavery.

The Hadith, another holy book of Islam, reveals more about Muhammad's character in a collection of thousands of traditions and stories passed down from that time. The following comes from *The Translation of the Meaning of Sahih Al-Bukhari* (Kazi Publications, Lahore, Pakistan, 1979) by Dr. Muhammad Muhsin Khan.

- Vol. 6, no. 435: Muhammad owned black slaves.
- Vol. 1, no. 90–91: Muhammad was short tempered.
- Vol. 2, no. 555; Vol. 3, no 391: Muhammad did not like questions about his claims to being a prophet or his revelations. "Allah has hated you . . . [for] asking too many questions." Vol. 1, no. 30: The Prophet told them repeatedly [in anger] to ask him anything they liked." But the people had learned not to ask anything.
- Vol. 7, no. 636: Muhammad was superstitious.[9]

Other Hadithic and Koranic sources expose his lack of a sense of humor, his sexual appetites, and his bitterness and hatred toward those who did not support his prophetic claims. He had 'Abdulla bin Ubai bin Salul killed for mistakenly accusing Aisha, one of Muhammad's wives, of adultery. When Muhammad "peacefully" invaded Mecca, supposedly without bloodshed, he had certain people killed who had written poems or songs that ridiculed him.

Mixed Manifestations

Muhammad may have fallen victim to human selfishness, but in a rough land full of division, chaos, idolatry, and bloodshed, he managed to bring the people into unity. He created a new, forceful world religion. This suggests he had a noble desire to see his people victorious.

We can only assume that Muhammad was convinced his calling was from God. Yet, he did not embody virtues that would clearly connect him with the God of the Bible. The man was manipulative, dishonest, greedy, covetous, self-seeking, violent, and a murderer. This mixture is what gave birth to the modern day religion of Islam; and this spirit of a wild warrior appears to have been passed from Muhammad to his descendents. Today, we see the same use of manipulation, treachery, deceit, and all manners of wicked terrorism to wreak havoc and force that religion on the lives of others.

Timeline: The Spread of Islam

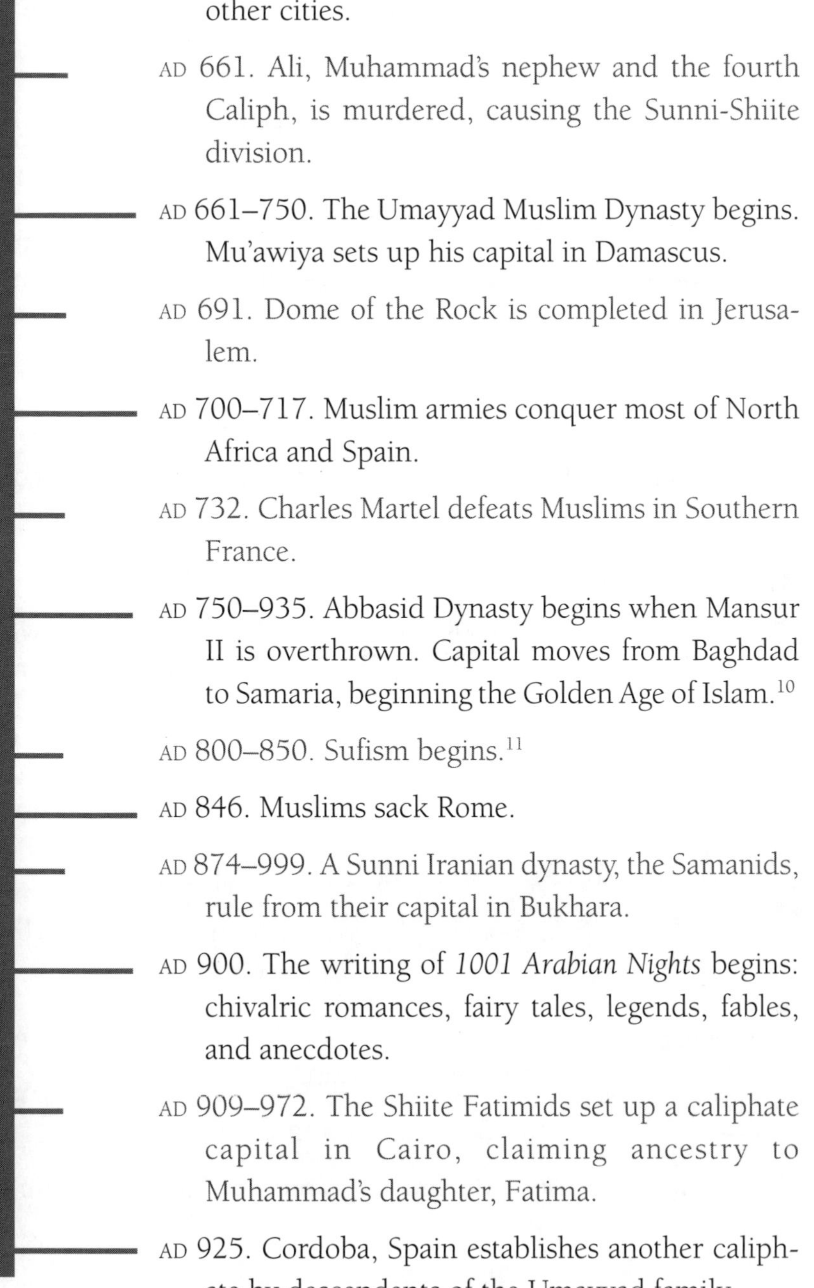

AD 637–38. Muslims capture Jerusalem and many other cities.

AD 661. Ali, Muhammad's nephew and the fourth Caliph, is murdered, causing the Sunni-Shiite division.

AD 661–750. The Umayyad Muslim Dynasty begins. Mu'awiya sets up his capital in Damascus.

AD 691. Dome of the Rock is completed in Jerusalem.

AD 700–717. Muslim armies conquer most of North Africa and Spain.

AD 732. Charles Martel defeats Muslims in Southern France.

AD 750–935. Abbasid Dynasty begins when Mansur II is overthrown. Capital moves from Baghdad to Samaria, beginning the Golden Age of Islam.[10]

AD 800–850. Sufism begins.[11]

AD 846. Muslims sack Rome.

AD 874–999. A Sunni Iranian dynasty, the Samanids, rule from their capital in Bukhara.

AD 900. The writing of *1001 Arabian Nights* begins: chivalric romances, fairy tales, legends, fables, and anecdotes.

AD 909–972. The Shiite Fatimids set up a caliphate capital in Cairo, claiming ancestry to Muhammad's daughter, Fatima.

AD 925. Cordoba, Spain establishes another caliphate by descendents of the Umayyad family.

Timeline (cont.): The Spread of Islam

AD 990–1118. The Seljûk Turkish family converts to Islam. Their war effort spreads the empire.

AD 1006. Muslims settle in India.

AD 1094. El Cid defeats Muslims in Spain.

AD 1095. Pope Urban II calls for a crusade against the invading Turks.

AD 1099. First Crusaders capture and sack Jerusalem.

AD 1187. Saladin defeats the Crusaders at the Battle of Hattin and restores Jerusalem to Islam.

AD 1224–1391. The Golden Horde Mongols convert to Islam and establish capital in Tabriz.

AD 1227. Genghis Khan, the Mongol leader, dies.

AD 1380–1699. Ottoman Turk Empire emerges with a capital in Bursa.

AD 1453. Muslims capture Constantinople and reestablish the capital as Istanbul. Remnants of the Ottoman Empire remain until the end of WWI.

AD 1503–1722. The Safavid Empire emerges.

AD 1526–1857. The Moghal Empire emerges when Babur, a Mongol leader, invades India.

AD 1571. Battle of Lepanto ends Muslim naval power in the Mediterranean.

AD 1654. Taj Mahal is completed.

AD 1669. Muslim rulers prohibit Hindu worship in India.

Timeline (cont.): The Spread of Islam

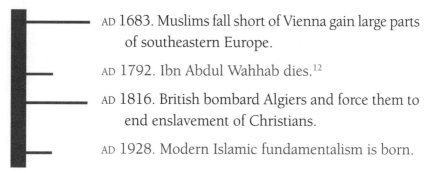

AD 1683. Muslims fall short of Vienna gain large parts of southeastern Europe.

AD 1792. Ibn Abdul Wahhab dies.[12]

AD 1816. British bombard Algiers and force them to end enslavement of Christians.

AD 1928. Modern Islamic fundamentalism is born.

CHAPTER 6

THE HISTORY OF ISLAM

Setting: AD 1453

Peter Ali Effendi stared after reacting swiftly to the actions of the priest. The stone floor in the sanctuary was slowly turning red. The scene was common in his life, but the haunting emotions inside were new. Slowly, he backed away from the fallen holy man whose only crime had been to try to close the door before the attacker got in.

Peter thought about his own parents. He could barely remember the cross that his father whittled for him, and his mother's kisses at night. He remembered his older brother, Timothy, playing with a stick sword as though he would conquer the Ottomans alone. But the raids became too frequent. His hometown was conquered and put under Muslim rule.

He remembered how the Muslims had treated his family. Ruthless men came to collect the tax known as the *devshirme*, where Christian subjects were forced to give their young sons into slavery for the Muslim army. It was a long time before he understood that his parents had to give him up or the entire family would have been executed.

Years of training in Muslim warfare as a Turkish Janissary had buried his sympathy for the Christians, but seeing this priest brought up the guilt he had felt during the invasion of Constantinople. The city was the last Christian bastion in the east. Mehmed II had used new, gunpowder weapons to annihilate the soldiers and guards at the city gates. Constantinople was quite a prize for Islam. After seeing the carnage, Peter held back in the attack. Other slave warriors could do the killing, not him.

Now, assigned to take his squad and secure St. Sophia's church until it could be converted to a mosque, he had done his duty. But he knew it wasn't right. He had sent his attachment to investigate all the rooms while he cleared the main sanctuary. That's when the surprised priest had rushed the door and fallen under Peter's lightening-fast sword.

"What is your name, assassin?"

Peter couldn't believe his ears. The priest was still alive. The young man peered into the dying man's face. "Peter. Peter Effendi is your assassin."

The priest narrowed his eyes in speculation. Then he realized the truth. In a voice of compassion he said, "Are you a part of the Janissaries?"

Peter nodded. "I am a slave-warrior. My parents were Christians. The Turks let me keep my birth name but replaced my father's name." The priest started to wheeze, gasping for air. Peter's heart broke. "I was startled and did not mean to stab you. I am so sorry."

The priest focused and looked into Peter's eyes. "Son, the Lord still loves you and wants your life. Turn again to Jesus, who died for you." Closing his eyes, he whispered, "Father, forgive him, for he did not know what he was doing."

As the rest of the squad finished their search and came into the sanctuary, each one saw the dead priest. Then their eyes turned to a lone Janissary at the front of the sanctuary, kneeling before the cross.

People often recast the history of Muhammad and Islam in a sympathetic light, one that does not include the warring or domineering spirit that was manifested. For instance, one historian said of Muhammad, "His surrender to God had been so complete that he had transformed society and enabled the Arabs to live together in harmony. The word *islam* is etymologically related to *salam* (peace), and in these early years Islam did promote cohesion and concord."[1]

Whatever "peace" Muhammad gained, it certainly wasn't peace for the Jews who were driven from their homes during his reign in Medina or those slaughtered by his sword. After he conquered Mecca, it is true that large numbers of Arab tribes sent emissaries to him and accepted Islam, but it is equally true that "others submitted only after military pressure."[2] It was also true that he forced those who would not become Muslims to submit to Islamic law and to pay taxes that Muslims did not have to pay. This was subtle coercion, even though the Koran would later forbid coercion in matters of faith (Sutra 2:256). The South Arabian Christians of Nejran not only submitted, but they had to pay a tribute of two thousand garments, each worth an ounce of silver, to enjoy the prophet's "protection."[3]

Muhammad was a charismatic individual, but he constantly struggled with those around him. As with Ishmael, his hand was against everyman's hand and everyman's hand was against his. As he died, about two years after conquering Mecca, peace had not truly been achieved. The wild spirit lived on in new, militant leaders.

The First Four Caliphs

Muhammad had no sons. Neither did he appoint any successors, though some held that he had appointed Ali, his cousin and son-in-law. After the prophet's death, his closest followers met together and elected Abu Bakr (632–634) as Caliph. He was one of the first converts to Islam and the father of Aisha, the beloved wife of Muhammad. His brief reign consisted largely of combat, mainly against those Arab tribes that decided to turn against Islam. These were known as the Ridda Wars, or the Wars of Apostasy. Of the first four caliphs, three were assassinated and all of them were involved in warfare and the aggressive expansion of Islam.

On his deathbed, Abu Bakr did not give the community the chance to elect a successor. He nominated Umar (634–644), who also spent his Caliphate in warfare. He conquered Damascus, Alexandria, Isfahan, and Jerusalem in 638 when the Christian ruler Sophronius surrendered.[4] As a teacher and practicing Muslim, Ruqaiyyah Maqsood pointed out the Islamic polemic approach in his book *Teach Yourself Islam*: "The formula was 'Islam, tribute, or sword', the sword being reserved for those who refused to cooperate and pay the appropriate taxes. Those who did convert to Islam lived tax-free."[5] In 644, Umar was assassinated by a disgruntled non-Muslim.[6]

The committee chose Uthman (644–656) as the third Caliph. During his reign the growing Muslim empire spread west across North Africa, and east to the border of China and the Indus Valley. Uthman had a bad reputation for promoting his own relatives to positions of power, so he died at the hand the Egyptians. His wife Nailah tried to protect him, but her fingers were cut off in the fight. She sent them along with her plea for help to Uthman's cousin, Mu'awiya, the Governor of Damascus in Syria.[7]

Twenty-four years after the prophet's death (656–661), Ali finally claimed to be the rightful successor. Aisha opposed his nomination. She said he was lax in justice and did not seek those who assassinated Uthman. Aisha led her army against Ali, beginning the first of several civil wars. She was captured at the Battle of Camel in 656 and was released to her friends in Madinah.

Also opposing Ali was Mu'âwiya; the Governor at Damascus because Ali did not go after the murderers of Uthman. Through negligence, it appeared as though Ali had supported the assassins. In AD 661, Mu'âwiya's army was strong in Arabia. Ali feared his own defeat, so he finally agreed to elections between himself and Mu'âwiya. However, this greatly offended some of Ali's own warriors because they thought he was the rightful Caliph. These warriors seceded from his ranks and created the Khârijites (Seceders). This group later assassinated Ali while he was praying.

Within just two decades after Muhammad's death, the Muslim armies had conquered land from Northern Africa to the Caucasus, and in the east beyond Iran to the Oxus River in present-day Afghanistan.[8] The rewards were plentiful. The once disunited bands of nomads who occasionally plundered a caravan were now a united horde of self-seeking, greedy, early Islamic fundamentalists. All for the "glory of Allah," the more they spread the faith of Islam, the more riches they gained by conquering villages and nations. The revenues from the lands they conquered were used as pensions for the descendents of Muhammad.[9]

Behind the fury of the Islamic storm that was spreading, a great schism was forming that would fracture the heart of the teachings and the people. The genuine adherents of the faith were dismayed because the noble side of Islamic teaching—equality, unity, community, serving Allah, and spreading the message—were being overshadowed by the baser elements of greed, power, lust, debauchery, and cruelty. Sin was always crouching at the door.

The Umayyad Dynasty (661–750)

The initial purpose of the Islamic Caliphate was to serve the cause and to spread the message of Islam. In reality, the Caliphate served the purposes of a small group of rich, powerful men that ruled by tyranny. When Mu'âwiya took control in AD 661, Islam took another step toward empowering a centralized autocracy, which continued to drain the influence of the Islamic community. In his book, *Islam in History*, Bernard Lewis points out the dilemma:

> By a tragic paradox, only the strengthening of the Islamic state could save the identity and cohesion of the Islamic community—and the Islamic state, as it grew stronger, moved further away from the social and ethical ideas of Islam. Resistance to this process of change was constant and vigorous, sometimes successful, but always unavailing—and out of this resistance emerged a series of religious sects, different in their ideologies and their support but alike in seeking to restore the radical dynamism that was being lost.[10]

During this time, two major sects began to emerge within Islam: the Sunnites and the Shiites. The Sunni followed the Caliphate, but the Shiites looked to the descendents of Ali as their spiritual leaders. This division caused more bloodshed and war within Islam.

During the ninety years of the Umayyad Dynasty, the Muslim armies conquered all of North Africa and captured Spain. Spain would remain Muslim for 700 years until the terrible Spanish Inquisition expelled it in 1492.

The Dome of the Rock was completed in Jerusalem in AD 691. It was the first major Islamic monument, and its completion informed the Christians—the majority—that Islam was there to stay.[11] However, the defeat of the Muslims in southern Europe by Charles Martel in 732 slowed their advances westward.

Within Islam, the Shiite revolutions were only one source of agitation. The converts to Islam, called *mawalis* (clients), were resentful second-class citizens. If they weren't Arabs, the difference was even greater. Also, Islam became more hostile toward Christians and other faiths. By AD 705, the church of Saint John at Damascus, which had been shared for Muslim and Christian worship, was completely taken over by the Muslims, and Arabic began to replace the traditional Greek.[12]

The Abbasid Dynasty (750–935)

The Abbasid faction capitalized on a widespread desire to see a descendent of Muhammad leading Islam. In AD 750, the last Umayyad Caliph, Mansur II in Iraq, was defeated. The new leader would be Abdallah, a descendent of the prophet's uncle Abbas.[13]

With advent of the new dynasty, some things in Muslim society improved while others got worse. Privilege of birth and race gradually gave way to more equal opportunity for all Muslims, not just Arab-Muslims. Commerce and the marketplace grew in both productivity and status. The streets of Baghdad—the new capital—bustled with business activity.

The Abbasid Dynasty also ushered in an advancement of science, medicine, mathematics, philosophy, and literature so that it became known as the Golden Age of Islam. This was the era of the writing of the 1001 Arabian Nights, a collection of numerous literary styles. Also written was Al Sufi's *Book of Fixed Stars*, which mentioned the astronomical concept of the nebula. In AD 900, the Arab physician Rhases became the first to describe smallpox, plague, and other infectious diseases. Later in the eleventh century, Avicenna (Ibn Sina) became the most influential Islamic medieval philosopher.[14]

According to Bernard Lewis, professor emeritus of Near Eastern Studies at Princeton University, the Umayyad Arab aristocrats were replaced by "the bureaucratic Abbasid state, with its well-ordered civil service and its professional army." Outwardly, they displayed all the trappings of Islamic piety, but inwardly they were more distant from Islamic ideals. Government became more complex and more oppressive—especially toward Christians.[15] Author Anne Cooper writes, "History records the forcible conversion of the 'last Christian tribe in Syria', the Banu Tanukh."[16] The Christians had been resisting Islam for many years and had often received help from the Byzantine emperor; but on the order of the Caliph al-Madhi (AD 775–785) they were required to become Muslims.

Muslims were constantly invading, conquering, and ransacking various communities outside their borders. In 856 AD the Muslims sacked Rome and the Vatican. Although they could not keep any foothold in that part of Europe, there were continual war parties scouting for more booty and land. During the Abbasid Dynasty, the Muslims did gain control of northern India and the area down to the Bay of Bengal.[17]

Within Islamic society, there was always the danger that some fanatic might invoke the Shariah (Islamic law) as an excuse for destroying Christian churches. The Caliph Harun-al Rashid ordered Christians and Jews to wear distinctive dress. This was fully in force by AD 807. Later, his grandson al-Mutawakkil restored these orders and added further decrees designed to humiliate Christians.

Near the end of the dynasty, changes were taking place across Islam. A Persian named Husayn Ibn Mansur Hallaj became a Sufi master and proclaimed that he—like Jesus Christ—was the "truth" and needed to be martyred for people's sin. Hallaj got his wish

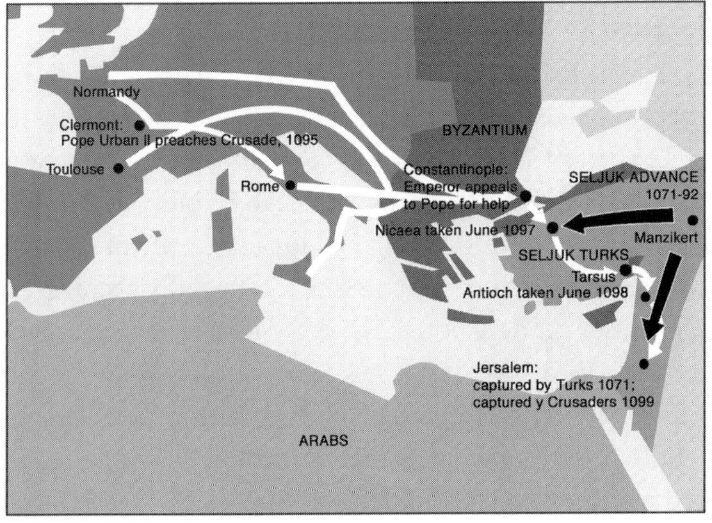

when he was blamed for a series of revolts and coups that broke out in Baghdad and was brutally executed.[18] Sufism, a mystical Islamic sect, grew as a result.

The Crusades

No other religion compares to the continual century-by-century military expansion of Islam. Muslims blame Christians for the Crusades, and rightfully so. But Christians can too easily point to a plethora of ancient atrocities by the Muslims, such as the massacre in the Moroccan city of Fez in the eighth century, where Islamic barbarians in the name of Allah intentionally slaughtered thousands of Christian families.[19]

When the Seljûk Turks captured Jerusalem in 1071, it sounded an alarm that a significant military response was necessary.[20] For too long the Muslims had gone unchecked, slaying Christians and taking territory by conquest without a significant military response. The Holy Land and the entire Western Empire was at stake.

Pope Urban II proclaimed the need for a Crusade in AD 1095, to regain the holy places of Christendom and the lands taken by the Muslims. Four years later, the Crusaders captured Jerusalem, but it eventually fell back into Muslim hands when Saladin defeated the Crusaders at the battle of Hattin in 1187. For almost two centuries the Muslims and Christians fought. The conquests were the most aggressive military campaigns that the Christians would ever use against the Muslims, and some of them were marked with great brutality.

Hindsight tells us that they were a great mistake. They brought reproach on the name of the Prince of Peace, Jesus Christ. They were not done by God's will or for His purpose. Yet, those who fought in them might disagree. The conflict did not develop in a vacuum or as a result of Christians converting to Islam. Author Karen Armstrong observes that, even though the wars were devastating for the Muslims of the Near East: "the vast majority of Muslims in Iraq, Iran,

Central Asia, Malaya, Afghanistan and Indiana" only knew of them as remote border wars.[21] Also, another source says, "The Muslims, unlike the Christians, did not regard the Crusades as something separate and distinctive, nor did they single out the Crusaders from the long series of infidel [non-Muslim] enemies whom from time to time they fought."[22]

Before the Crusades ended, Christian missionaries, acting in the true character of the faith, went forth in peace to preach the gospel. During the Fifth Crusade, Francis of Assisi went to share his faith with the Sultan of Egypt. Later the same year, five Franciscan monks were martyred in Morocco. Within a hundred years, another missionary, Raymond Lull, took the gospel message to Tunis, Africa, where he also was martyred.[23]

Early in the twentieth century, when the West began eclipsing the Muslim nations with military power, Muslim historians became preoccupied with the medieval Crusades, wishing for another Saladin to arise.[24] As a result, the Crusades have become the modern justification for irrational Islamic fundamental warfare. What seems to be ignored by sympathetic historians is the fact that Islamic warriors of the seventh and eighth centuries invaded all parts of Christendom and advanced into Spain, Portugal, southern Italy, and France.

Still, during the 1990s, Christians traveled to Europe and the Near East to walk the paths of the Crusaders in a series of "reconciliation walks." As they went, Christians asked forgiveness of Muslims and Jews for the historical atrocities that took place in the name of Jesus Christ. Many amazing testimonies surfaced, like those of my wife's Aunt Linda, who went on two of these walks. She saw some Muslims rejoice and weep in gladness that the Christians were asking forgiveness for the ancient past. Others could not conceive why modern Christians felt the need to repent. She had numerous opportunities to pray with Muslims for a peace and an understanding of the truth.

The Great Islamic Empires

Historians indicate that a steady infusion of nomadic people from the Turkish steppe area gave Islam access to fresh leadership and greater military prowess. The continual conquest and advancement of Islam funneled its followers into combat with many types of people. The unspoiled virtues of new nomadic converts kept the corrupting influences of the empire in check.[25] The Turkish Seljûks, Egyptian Mamluks, Asian Mongols, and Anatolian Ottomans all brought a fresh vitality for conquest and dominance.

Hulagu, the grandson of Mongol Chieftain Genghis Khan, invaded India in 1258 with his Mongol army of nomads and conquered all in his path. The last Abbasid Caliph fell to them in Baghdad. It wasn't until 1260 that the Mongols were stopped in Palestine. Mongol conversions then added fresh vision to conquest.

The rise of the Ottoman, Safavid, and Moghal Empires took the Islamic faith and concept of state to new levels of strength and influence. The Ottoman Empire, which started in the thirteenth century in northwest Anatolia, conquered Syria, Iraq, the Balkans, Egypt, the Red Sea area, and laid siege to Vienna twice. In 1453, Mehmed II conquered the Christian bastion of Constantinople by using new gunpowder weaponry. This was renamed Istanbul and became the new capital. Further, they turned St. Sophia Basilica into a mosque. The Ottoman Empire remained strong until the Treaty of Karlowitz in 1699. Vestiges of the empire lasted until the end of World War I.

The Safavid (1503–1722) and Moghal Empires (1526–1857) did not last as long as the Ottoman, but each was important in establishing Islam. In the Safavid Empire, Shâh Abbas quenched the political feuding while successfully restructuring the institutions of the Islamic state. In the Moghal Empire, a Mongol army invaded India near Dehli and eventually took the entire part of southern India. Shâh Jehân built the majestic Taj Mahal in 1654 as a tomb for himself and his favorite wife. As with the many previous

The Three Muslim Empires

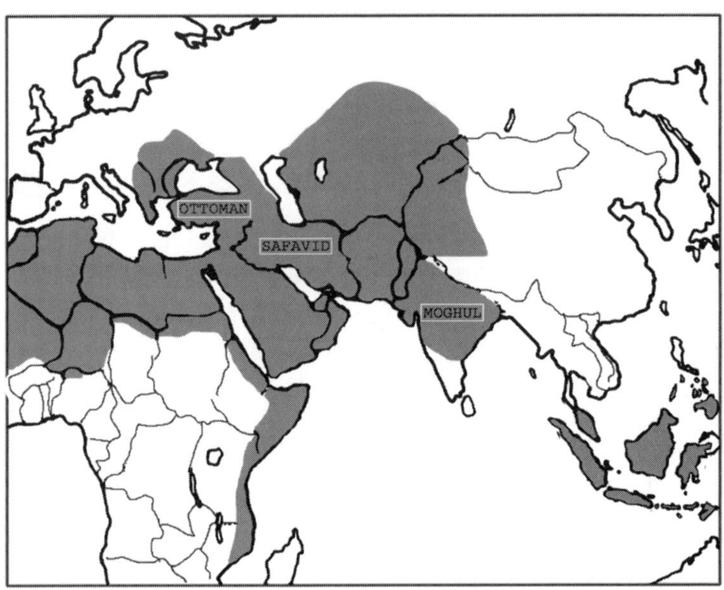

examples, Islam once again showed intolerance in 1669 by prohibiting Hindu worship. Later, in nineteenth century Iran, thousands of adherents to the Baha'i cult were slaughtered for espousing their religious beliefs.

Over time, the evolving cultural and technological advances of the West gradually created a wide gulf between itself and the Islamic religious culture that preferred to hold on to the past. The weapons of the West soon controlled the battles. In 1571, the naval Battle of Nepanto ended any Muslim naval activities in the Mediterranean Sea. In 1816, the superior British armory bombarded Algiers and forced them to end the enslavement of Christians. European colonialism and dominance became inevitable. The Great Empires had fallen.

The Modern Empire

The recent history of Islamic fundamentalism began in eighteenth century Arabia by an alliance of Muhammad ibn Abd al-Wahhab, a fundamentalist preacher, to Muhammad ibn Saud, a militant chief of the house of Saud. Since early in Islamic history, Arabia had not been the center seat of Islam. Ibn Wahhab desired to see Islam purified, returned to the religion of the prophet, with Mecca and Medina restored to their rightful place in Islam. However, few converts joined from his preaching until he allied with a warrior who had ambition for power. Through military and terrorist activities they brought many converts to Ibn Wahhab's view of Islam. The adherents of Wahhabism prefer to be called *Unitarians*. Two hundred and fifty years have passed since then and Saudi Arabia is still ruled by Saudi monarchy, the Koran, and puritan dogma. From Ibn Wahhab's teachings sprouted the present Wahhabism movement throughout Islam known as fundamentalism. [26] The great difference between then and now are the potency of the weapons.

In his book, *Crisis in Belief*, Bishop Stephen Neill points out the incredible transformation of Islamic power in the last century:

> In two generations the situation of the Islamic World has entirely changed. In 1918 it was at its lowest point of humiliation—poor, exhausted, and at almost every point subject to Christian domination. In 1978 it stood before the world, free, aggressive, and with a new sense of confidence.[27]

Since WWII many Islamic nations have gained their independence. European colonialism ended, and the new countries faced an identity crisis that continues to this day to produce bloodshed, rebellion, and great social upheaval. A portion of the continued crisis is caused by the extremist views of Islamic fundamentalists.

PART THREE

TENETS OF THE FAITH

——— ✡ ✞ ☪ ———

CHAPTER 7

RITUALS AND BELIEFS

Setting: Konya, Turkey; 1870.

Hassan Ali watched the men dance in a circle. His eyes drifted from their black gowns to the sign up above: THE ORDER OF THE WHIRLING DERVISHES. He turned to Khâlid, his friend, and said, "I am impressed, but what does it symbolize?"

"Just watch." After the last dervish kissed the hand of the pîr stationed in the center of the dancers, the dervishes in one accord threw off their black gowns and revealed white ones underneath. The audience cheered as the dancers whirled on axis in a seemingly endless motion.

Khâlid leaned back and said, "I read that the black gowns of these Sufi dancers represent their earthly bodies; and white, their heavenly eternal ones. When Jalaluddin Rumi created this dance 600 years ago, the dancers represented the circular motion of the soul in the Sufi's love for and complete attention to God." Shortly after, the young men left the building and walked toward the inn. Both contemplated the powerful music, poetry, and dancing.

"Okay," said Hassan, "I admit that the Sunni way seems like mere obedience to Allah. We recite the Shahadah, pray, give, fast, and do everything to simply obey him. Is the Shiite way better? Your teachers are strict, and they tell you the savior Mahdi will return. Yet, the Bab identified himself as Mahdi and he was executed. Later, Bahá'u'lláh claimed the same and was exiled. Why do you continue to wait?"

Khâlid had heard the argument before. "Hassan, most the Iranian Shiites I knew in the shipping industry discerned that the claims of the Bab and Bahá'u'lláh were false. However, I did not endorse the persecution of their followers. The Shah did that on his own, all for political gain. I search for the truth, not the movements of a crowd. Can the emptiness in my heart be filled with the greatness of Allah, or must I just obey him?"

"Well, return to Istanbul tomorrow and join the Dervishes." Hassan tried to lighten the mood. "Your wives would love the mystical dances of the Sufi."

Khâlid thought a moment. "But not the poverty. Besides, Sufi ways are really bizarre. Magical amulets and séances give me the creeps. And how can music and poetry teach me more about Allah?"

"Like Christian monks, the Divershes live outside the norm to truly seek and know Allah. That's why it's a dangerous path to follow: You may end up embracing Christianity itself."

There are five basic pillars of Islam that drives Muslim life. The simplicity of these personal obligations has given this religion its growing appeal. Christians should understand these pillars. Cultural sensitivity is critical for reaching the Muslims in the community—and around the world.

Five Pillars of Islam

1. TO RECITE THE SHAHADAH

The shortest religious creed in the world is the creed of Islam:

There is no god but Allah and Muhammad is his messenger.

Repeating a phrase does not make it true, but it has been proven as an effective means of brainwashing or mentally conditioning individuals. Devout Muslims recite this constantly. The words are whispered into the ears of a newborn infant, are repeated throughout his life, and are often the last words spoken before death. The words are used for the call to prayer five times a day, and are a comfort at moments of crisis.[1] It's the mental foundation for Islamic life, spoken so often that it becomes ingrained into the thought and belief systems and challenges any alternative thinking.

The Shahadah is also used at conversion. According to Maqsood, when someone utters these words before two witnesses and truly believes the words in his heart, he has entered the faith. The proof is seen in the individual's changed life and adherence to the Shariah, or Islamic law. The person must not eat pork or other forbidden animal products. They are to give up alcohol, entertainment based upon the social aspects of alcohol, and immodest dress. Furthermore, they are to give up arrogance, selfishness, deceitfulness, and other character weaknesses.[2]

2. TO PRAY (*SALAT*)

Symbolizing the five steps of Muhammad on the night of his ascent into the seven heavens, prayers are performed five times a day—dawn, noon, mid-afternoon, dusk, and two hours after sunset.[3] Men and women are to be clean and modestly dressed. Women should not wear makeup or perfume. Often using a prayer mat, adherents face toward Mecca in a ritual called *qiblah*. They remove their shoes, then stand, kneel, bow, lay prostrate, and repeat certain suras.

Once a week, on Fridays at noon, Muslim men are expected to attend the mosque. Sometimes believers carry prayer beads, similar to the Catholic rosary. The 99 beads represent the 99 revealed names of Allah. The worshipper repeats "Glory be to Allah. Thanks be to Allah. God is Most Great" 33 times each as he or she passes over the beads.[4]

3. TO GIVE ALMS (*ZAKAT*)

One-fortieth (2.5%) of a Muslim's income is considered an alms tax that must be given to the poor.

4. TO FAST DURING RAMADAN (*SAWM*)

The highest of holy seasons is the Muslim's ninth month. In honor of Muhammad receiving the Koran during this month, fasting is required every day during sunlight hours. They must abstain from eating, drinking, smoking, and sexual intercourse.[5]

5. TO MAKE THE PILGRIMAGE TO MECCA (*HAJJ*)

Muslims are expected to go to Mecca at least once in their lifetime and pay homage to Allah at the temple. Currently, about two million Muslims go each year. There are two types of pilgrimages. The smaller one does not correspond with specific dates. It is called *'umra*.

The second kind of pilgrimage is taken during Dhu l-hijjah, the last month of the Islamic moon calendar. *Hajj* is the honorary title for those who go to Mecca on the great pilgrimage. Pilgrims do not shave, comb their hair, use perfume, or cut nails and hair. They cannot hunt, argue, or have sexual intercourse.[6] Dressed in standardized white garments and sandals to diminish class distinction, pilgrims try to see or—if fortunate enough—touch and kiss the Black Stone, a bowling ball-sized object, possibly of meteoric origin, that is set in a silver collar in a corner of the Kabah.[7]

The Kabah in Mecca has been the central shrine of Islam since AD 624. Approximately fifty feet high, it lies in the middle of the Grand Mosque as an empty windowless room with marble walls. At the east corner, the Black Stone is embedded into the wall about five feet above the ground. Its surface has been polished smooth by centuries of contact with hands and lips. The outer walls of the *bayt Allah* ("House of God") are hung with a black brocade blanket (*kiswah*). Embroidered on the brocade in gold thread are numerous Koranic verses. Each year, the $4.5 million covering is replaced with a new one in a festival ritual.[8]

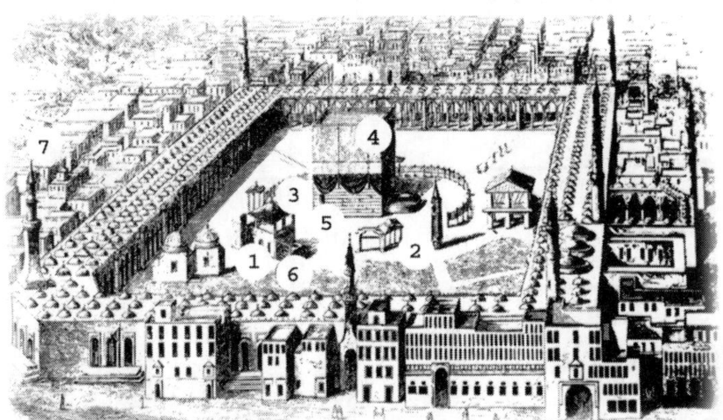

The Grand Mosque of Mecca (in the 19th Century)

1. The well of Zamzam.
2. The place of Abraham.
3. The Matâf, the open area to walk around the Ka'bah.
4. The Ka'bah.
5. Entrance to the Ka'bah and the Black Stone.
6. Stairs to the water taps of the Zamzam well.
7. Path on which pilgrams run several times (sa'y) between Safâ and Marwah.

What Is the Holy Jihad?

Considered by some to be the sixth pillar of the faith, *jihad* is the center of many debates. Additional controversy has arisen since the September 11th attack on America. Author Anne Cooper explains it as meaning "to struggle to the utmost of one's capacity." Various interpretations exist:

- A holy war and defense of Islam
- Raiding and conquest during the early spread of Islam
- A modern call to propagate Islam
- Personal self-disciple.[9]

Jihad literally means "efforts on God's path," but it is roughly translated as "holy war." Accordingly, a jihad is supposed to be primarily an inner struggle rather than a military one. Yes, there are Muslims who consider the greatest jihad to be the struggle with one's own heart, the attempt to bring oneself in accord with the will of God. The various means to fight this struggle are prayer, study, and various forms of inner-worldly asceticism.[10]

There are large Christian populations in Egypt, Syria, and Lebanon.

At one time in history, a jihad could be an offensive or defensive war. An offensive jihad was supposed to be lead by a legitimate successor to the prophet. Since none exists today, that tenet indicates that the jihad should only be defensive in nature.[11]

Islamic fundamentalists twist that idealism by reasoning that the best defense is a good offense. They say they have taken up arms to defend Islam against the influences of the West. No place outside of Islam is safe.

After the September 11th attack, various Muslim leaders appeared on television to temper that view. They denied that a militant jihad was part of Islamic teaching. Most were American Muslims who do not speak for the majority of Muslims outside the United States. A friend of mine noticed, "The silence of the international Islamic leaders on the subject of the Islamic jihad in relationship to the modern offensiveness of the fundamentalists is deafening." American Muslims don't have a violent, militant, offensive, or even fundamental view of the jihad. They appreciate the freedoms they have in the United States. Plus, they don't want neighbor Americans to think that Islam could have nasty doctrines like that of a justified holy war.

But it does.

Muslims cannot deny the overt militant application of the jihad. Muhammad led the first one. Afterward, a series of jihads broadened Islamic influence across the Middle East, including Jerusalem, which was under Christian control. The conquests continued west into Africa, east into Asia, and penetrated Europe three times.

In his book, *In the Shadow of the Prophet: Struggle for the Soul of Islam,* Milton Viorst writes: "Muslims, from Islam's earliest days, were bound by the Prophet's precedent to wage jihad, 'holy war' to promote the faith. The very name given to the non-Islamic world—Dar al-Harb, the 'domain of war'—reaffirmed this duty. But over the centuries the religious scholars have softened the duty, thereby enabling Islam to coexist with its diverse neighbors."[12]

Author Bernard Lewis was interviewed in the *Wall Street Journal* shortly after the September attack. He noted that jihad goes beyond a spiritual and moral struggle. "The more common interpretation, and that of the overwhelming majority of the classical jurist and commentators, presents jihad as an armed struggle for Islam against infidels and apostates. Unlike 'crusade' it has maintained its religious and military connotation into modern times."[13]

This was the reason behind Osama bin Laden's 1998 declaration against the United States.

The Six Major Doctrines

1. GOD

There is one true God, Allah, who is all seeing, all knowing, all-powerful. If someone associates a partner with God, it is an unforgivable sin called *shirk*. Sura 4:51, "Verily, God will not forgive the union of other gods with Himself."[14] Thus, the Christian teaching of the Trinity is offensive to Muslims.

2. ANGELS

The chief angel is Gabriel, who is said to have appeared to Muhammad. There is also a fallen angel named Shaitan (from the Hebrew, Satan). His followers are the jinn (demons).[15] These jinn are where the concept of the genie comes from. It is also believed that each person has two angels in life: one recording the good deeds, and one the bad.

3. HOLY BOOKS

Five holy books are mentioned in the Koran:

1. The scrolls of Abraham, which are now lost
2. The Tawrat (the Torah), given to the prophet Moses
3. The Zabur (the Psalms), given to the prophet David
4. The Injil (the Gospels), given to the prophet Jesus
5. The Koran, which was revealed to the prophet Muhammad

The Hadith is also sacred to Muslims but not mentioned in the Koran. It was written later. Muslims believe that the Bible is badly corrupted. The Koran supersedes all previous revelations and is Allah's final revelation.

4. THE PROPHETS

Muhammad is the greatest of the 26 prophets mentioned in the Koran.[16] Tradition suggests that there have been 124,000 prophets who have visited various cultures throughout history, bringing the true teachings of monotheism and Allah.[17]

5. THE END TIMES

On the Day of Judgment, Allah will reward or punish people according to their deeds. The results will be heaven or hell. The concept of heaven is referred to a little. Sura 55 indicates that it will be quite a place—for men, that is—full of beautiful women, pillowed couches, flowing fountains, and plenty of fruit to eat in luscious gardens of pleasure.

The Koran majors much on the subject of hell. It is mentioned in almost every sura.

6. PREDESTINATION

Orthodox (Sunni) Islam is fatalistic, a pessimistic worldview. Devout Muslims constantly make decisions with the comment "If Allah wills it" because orthodox Islam teaches the absolute predestination of both good and evil. All thoughts, words, and deeds, whether good or evil, were foreseen, foreordained, determined, and decreed from all eternity. Everything that happens takes place according to what has been written for it.[18]

Orthodox Islam also denies the ability to freely choose or reject Allah. This extreme view of predestination causes a lot of theological controversy, even among Muslims, because it creates natural contradictions within the Koran and eliminates human responsibility. At that point, God becomes the author of both good *and* evil, which some have used to justify pantheism.

The Sects of Islam

There have been many schisms within Islam. At the time of the prophet, differences were solved by military muscle and

Muhammad's revelation. The prophet's army won the battles and his revelations were the law. After Muhammad's death, the caliphs created divisions. Today, the Sunnis and Shiites have become the two major sects of modern Islam. Eventually, the Sufi emerged. A simplified and general way of considering the three is this:

- Sunni are orthodox, led by majority consensus
- Shiites are radical, led by specific authority
- Sufi are mystical, led by individual quest

THE SUNNITES (SUNNI)

This moderate, orthodox sect of Islam comprises approximately 80% of the believers.[19] They focus on the traditions of Islam. *Sunnah* means "customs."

Author Ruqaiyyah Maqsood says, "The life and example of the Prophet are known as the Sunnah."[20] Also included are the teachings of the Koran and Hadith, and also the teachings of subsequent religious scholars throughout history. The consensus of these scholars is often considered to be the will of God. The Sunni have a tendency to separate religion from politics.

THE SHIITES (SHIAS)

This radical arm comprises about 10%–15% of Islam. Originally, they disagreed with Sunnis on who should rule Islam after Muhammad died. The Sunni accepted the four caliphs that succeeded Muhammad. They were considered the best men in the community to lead, regardless of their kinship with Muhammad. Shiites believed that only a member of Muhammad's own family should succeed him. Since he had no son, it was thought that the only rightful successor was Ali, the prophet's cousin and the husband of Fatima, a daughter of Muhammad. These specially appointed family leaders were called *imams*. According to the Shiites, these political and spiritual rulers of Islam were infallible vessels of God's light. Today, Shiites add to the creed of Islam the words "and Ali is the friend of God."[21]

After Ali was assassinated in AD 661, the party of 'Ali (Arabic shi'at 'Ali) was formed. The Shiites disavowed the Umayyad family and recognized Ali's son Hasan as leader. But Hasan had no ambition, so they acknowledged his younger brother, Husayn, as imam. On October 10, in the year 680, soldiers of the Umayyad Caliph massacred Ali and a small group in the Iraqi desert of Kerbala. Husayn had been deserted by many of the Shiites. Today, the Shiites mourn for that sin on October 10th every year.

After Husayn, other imams were recognized, but eventually it caused another schism. Today, there are:

- Fiver Shiites (Zaydites)—moderates that elect descendents of 'Ali to lead them
- Sevener Shiites (Ishmailites)—esoteric and full of strife
- Twelver Shiites (Imamites)—the largest group, these people have "a strong desire for salvation," thinking that the twelfth imam is the savior who will come out of hiding at the end of time[22]

The Shiite salvation concept bucks against the Sunni belief of predestination. Shiites believe in free choice. In addition, upon the return of the twelfth imam, Mahdi, he is expected to establish a divine kingdom of justice. Consequently, Shiites question the legitimacy of earthly political power.

Amazingly, Sunnis regard Shiites with disdain. They see them as intolerant, speculative extremists who preach revolution, martyrdom, and terrorism. Shiites embrace the militant interpretation of jihad and call the West "the Great Satan."[23] The Ayatollah Khomeini of Iran was a Shiite leader who spoke out against the West. Shiites currently have large percentages of population in Iran (91%), Azerbaijan (70%), Iraq (62%), Bahrain (50%), Yemen (47%), Lebanon (40%), Afghanistan (30%), Kuwait (25%), and Pakistan (15%).[24]

THE SUFI

Sufism has Gnostic and Pantheistic tendencies. Sufis are not concerned about traditional Islam or monotheism, but often practice animism and spiritism.

Many conservative Muslims reject this mystical sect of Islam. In their book *Tales from the Land of the Sufis*, Mojdeh Bayet and Mohammad Ali Jamnia teach that Sufism has two major concepts: the unity of being—a concept that the universe is a manifestation of God's attributes and, as such, is not separate from Him—and the order of Sufi masters, who provide guidance for people who are seeking God.[25]

While orthodox Islam is concerned about ultimate truth, the nature of reality, and the way to heaven, Sufism is more concerned about day-to-day living and whatever works in the pursuit of God. An example could be "A father with a sick son will ask the mullah to pray to God for him, tie an amulet to his arm to drive off evil spirits and give him modern medicine to kill the germs, all at the same time."[26]

The Shariah

The Shariah is the general title for Islamic law—the foundation from Allah for all creation. More than a legal system, the Shariah is based on obligations found in the Koran that can guide people to walk in Allah's will. The Shariah addresses 50 major areas of one's life, including religious practices, family law, inheritance, trade, customs, traditions, and civil and criminal law. It even includes such things as greetings, dress, and what to say to someone who sneezes. Whereas Christians *model* their lives after Jesus, Muslims *require* this conduct. Faithfulness to the law determines one's eternal destiny in heaven or hell.[27]

For the first 300 years after Muhammad's death, Islamic jurists argued about the many religious and legal aspects of the Koran and the Hadith. When Muhammad died, the so-called law was only a hodge-podge of rules and admonitions. Thinking that they needed a comprehensive system, the jurists divided and created four Sunni schools of Shariah Law:

- The liberal school of the Hanafites
- The moderate school of the Shafiites
- The uncompromising, dogmatic school of the Hanbalites
- The school of the Malikites, based primarily on seventh-century community practices in Medina
- The Jafarites

This Shiite Jafarite school of Law teaches that religious leaders can interpret divine law (God's Will) anew. The Sunnis disagree and believe that no new interpretation is available since the tenth century.

Leading Shiite imams can earn the title *ayatollah,* or "shadow of God." Thus, the Ayatollah Khomeini acted in accordance with Allah's law when he overthrew the pro-Western Shaw Muhammad Reza Pahlevi in 1979. Before the revolution, Khomeini wrote the following in exile:

> The entire system of government and administration, together with the necessary laws, lies ready for you. If the administration of the country calls for taxes, Islam has established them provision; and if laws are needed, Islam has established them all. There is no need for you after establishing a government, to sit down and draw up laws, or, like rulers who worship foreigners and are

> infatuated with the West, run after others to borrow their laws. Everything is ready and waiting. All that remains is to draw up ministerial programs, and that can be accomplished with the help and cooperation of consultants and advisers who are experts in different fields, gathered together in a consultative assembly.[28]

Was Khomeini's experiment of the Islamic state successful? No. When he returned and overthrew the Shaw, a half a million Iranian professionals fled the country; ten thousand people—including women and children—were executed; and rebellion, intervention, and war cost Iran a half a million lives and two million refugees.[29] Is it any wonder that the Iranians elected the moderate cleric Mohammed Khatami in May 1997 by a clear 70%? The concept of the Islamic state under Shariah law had failed.[30]

Unfortunately, many other nations are struggling to bring the Shariah into a place of absolute law. Persecution and intolerance is currently manifesting to many of those citizens. In Indonesia, the rise of fundamentalist and militant groups is forcing women to wear headscarves. They also raid hotel rooms to validate proof of marriage. Alcohol and discotheques are forbidden.[31] Author Milton Viorst says, "Fundamentalism has remained on the agenda, not only among the Arabs but among Muslims everywhere. Clearly, most Muslims feel less threatened by their fundamentalism than most Christians and Jews feel by theirs. If fundamentalism is to win out among any of the 'Abrahamic' faiths—Judaism, Christianity, and Islam are all said to descend from the patriarch Abraham—it will surely have its first triumph in Islam."[32]

CHAPTER 8

THE KORAN

Setting: Near Mecca, in the middle of the seventh century.

"No," he said defiantly, "Muhammad did not say 'we' or 'us.' I wrote it right here." Ali held up the ancient shoulder bone to the firelight. "He distinctly said 'he.' We've discussed this before. How could Allah be described as 'we' or 'us'? Nobody has ever agreed with you on this subject. Your verses have other glaring mistakes as well."

Zaid walked around the other side of the fire and leaned close to Ali's face. "I told you. I was there. Some of these men have confirmed it. I heard the Prophet as well as you. And I wrote it down."

"You wrote yours down on a palm leaf three weeks after I did. Then fire ruined part of it! Mine was right after the Prophet spoke, and is still intact."

Zaid was incredulous. "So what? It was two months before you wrote it on that bone. So time can't be that big of a deal to you. Besides, Abdallah agrees with me, and he wrote his a week or so before yours."

The whole group erupted. Finally, Ali got his voice above the clamor. "Zaid, don't you know? Abdallah wasn't even *there* when the Prophet spoke it. He wrote what Nailah told him, and she's changed her mind twice on what that was. Besides, Muhammad's favorite, Ayesha, thinks it should always be 'he' and not 'we' or 'us.'"

Uthman came to Zaid's rescue. "Well, the words 'we' or 'us' are used in other Koranic verses describing Allah." But Ali didn't care.

"What? So, Uthman, are we simply to reason this way every time we disagree. Aren't we supposed to examine each verse in the light of its evidence? Was the Koran merely committed to men's faulty memory? Here is something actually written down and you differ with its context. Many have never agreed with the other verses that said 'we' or 'us.' Now, you want everyone simply to ignore what we've actually written down. Must all future generations blindly accept your inventions? Or should they make it up too?

Uthman was visibly angry. "Watch it." Ali shrugged.

"This sounds like an argument for the satanic verses." The group exploded. Men yelled wildly at each other while waving portions of papyrus, bones, stones, and sticks—each one a proclamation from the Prophet. Others, who had no writings, defended what they remembered.

No one saw the rider approach, but a piercing whistle quieted the crowd. After dismounting, the man walked to the fire and said, "I bring a message from Caliph Umar. Tomorrow we ride against Jerusalem and take it from the infidel Christians. They have refused to pay tribute. Our jihad will gain the holy city where Muhammad was led by Gabriel into heaven on his night visitation."

Afterward, only Ali stood silent. The rest turned their attentions to the battle—and the loot. Ali was troubled by so many inaccuracies in what the Prophet had said. Was this what Allah wanted? Why worry about accuracy and reason? Most of the men didn't really care anyway. He turned the shoulder bone over in his hand, already regretting what he was about to do. He hoped someday Allah would convict this self-righteous, gullible bunch. Looking around, he checked the area and then quickly dropped the bone in the fire.

"Give not way to the infidels, but by means of this Koran strive against them with a mighty strife" (Sura 25:54). Muhammad used the pen and the sword to bring influence, but certainly it was his pen that changed the world.

The word *Koran* means "to recite." According to Islamic tradition, the Koran was revealed to Muhammad by the angel Gabriel between the years AD 610–632. Scribes wrote the revelations down on everything from pieces of papyrus to stones, palm leaves, shoulder bones, animal ribs, leather, and boards.[1] All of those were collected after his death. Soon, numerous versions were circulating among the population. Caliph Uthman caused great controversy by authorizing one version and having many of the rest destroyed. This version became the Koran. The other versions that survived show variants of individual suras and verses. This has caused a scholarly debate within modern Islam, but it has also closed the ancient manuscripts to Western scholastic criticism.[2]

Sura 13:37 reads that the Koran is "a code in the Arabic tongue." Hence, Arabic was the perfect language of the Koran and any other translation would simply be an interpretation.[3] Interestingly, author Arthur Jeffrey, in his book *The Foreign Vocabulary of the Quran*, cites more than 100 foreign non-Arabic words in the Koran.[4] The suras (chapters) are not in chronological order and are without organization. The first one was probably Sura 96:

Recite thou, in the name of thy Lord who created;—
Created man from clots of blood:—
Recite thou! For thy Lord is the most Beneficent,
Who hath taught the use of the pen;—
Hath taught Man that which he knoweth not. (Sura 96:1–5)

Muhammad was familiar with Bible stories, even though he called himself the "unlettered Prophet" in Sura 7:156 and adamantly denied that he received any information from outside sources. The translator J. M. Rodwell, in his commentarial notes on the Koran, wrote: "There can, however, be no doubt that Muhammad—in spite of assertions to the contrary, with the view of proving his inspiration—was well acquainted with the Bible stories."[5] Rodwell considers Muhammad to be sincere in his quest but ultimately "self-deceived."[6]

The Koran consists of 114 suras and 6666 verses, known as *ayas* (meaning "signs"). Each is thought to be a sign from God.[7] The most popular tradition divides the suras into four periods:

- Early Meccan
- Middle Meccan
- Late Meccan
- Medinan[8]

After the first sura, there was an intermission of six months to three years. During this time is when Muhammad struggled with whether or not the revelations and voices were from God. He debated with people who thought he was demon possessed. Suras 7:181 and 81:20–29 show that people, even companions, thought his doctrine was from Satan. In sura 69:40–47 Muhammad demands that he is an apostle and not a poet. The jinn were believed to inspire the poets.[9] Still, the strong possibility of demonic influence was demonstrated by his:

1. Concern over the seizures
2. Manipulation of the revelations for his own gain
3. Dishonesty in the Koranic sources
4. Brutality toward those who did not embrace his message
5. Spirit of warfare against Christians and Jews

The Arabs of the day obviously had a problem with his assertions of the Koran's divine inspiration. For example, in Sura 3:181 Muhammad defends himself against being called a liar by proclaiming that he is an apostle. In Sura 67:9, he imagines himself in heaven on Judgment Day, hearing the voices of those who did not believe him. The unbelievers are then forced to confess that they thought he was a liar and full of delusion. Below are a few verses that, by extrapolation, reveal obvious Arab resistance and rebuttal to his message:

> But when our clear signs are recited to them, they who look not forward to meet Us, say, "Bring a different Koran from this, or make some change in it." (Sura 10:16)

> This is no new fiction, but a confirmation of previous scriptures, and an explanation of all things, and guidance and mercy to those who believe. (Sura 12:111)

> And the infidels say, "The Koran is a mere fraud of his own devising, and others have helped him with it, who had come hither by outrage and lie." And they say, "Tales of the ancients that he hath put in writing! And they were dictated to him morn and even." (Sura 25:5–6)

It is evident that people did not like what Muhammad was saying. They also apparently accused him of writing fiction, making up fraudulent stories, and borrowing writings from ancient sources. This is not easy criticism to take when one is trying to convince people of a divine revelation from heaven.

> Will they say, 'He hath forged it (the Koran) himself?' Nay, rather it is that they believed not. Let them produce a discourse like it, if they speak the Truth. (Sura 52:32–33)

> Then bring a Sura like it; and call on whom ye can beside God, if ye speak truth. (Sura 10:39)

Some took Muhammad up on his challenge. Nadir ibn Haritha arranged some stories of Persian kings into suras and recited them.[10] Hamzah ben-Ahed wrote a book against the Koran. Another man, Maslema, wrote a book that caused "a defection of great number of Mussulmans."[11]

Remember, Muhammad did have a commitment for driving out any worship other than that of his tribe's god, Allah. He also wanted to bring unity to the scattered Arab tribes and be their leader. Yet, that does not necessarily mean he had God's approval, character, or inspiration.

The Perfect Tablet

The Koran displays a passion on behalf of Muhammad for Allah, such as in mercy and compassion. Muhammad appreciates the plight of the poor and tries to alleviate their burden. There are admonitions toward high moral standards. He also improves the standards and rights of women, but did not see them as equals. He confirmed the inferiority of women in Arabian society in sura 4:37–38, pronouncing that men have the right to "scourge' wives who are disobedient. The Koran also endorses polygamy of up to four wives.

Some suras appear to promote peace and good will between Arabs and their non-Muslim neighbors. Those must have been revealed during the early years, when he hoped to influence the Jews, Christians, and rebellious Arabs by his entreaties. However, by the end, he was a full-fledged warrior-prophet.

The Koran is supposedly the *umm al-kittab*, the preexistent scripture preserved in heaven. It was uncreated. Muhammad said: "Yet it is a glorious Koran, written on the preserved Tablet" (Sura 85:21–22). But the Mu'tazilites of the ninth century, a body of dissident theologians, challenged this thinking by teaching that only Allah was uncreated because he has existed forever; therefore, the Koran must be created.[12] Yet, Muslim consensus has not embraced this view and still holds that the Koran is "eternal, uncreated, and perfect."[13]

Numerous narratives in the Koran reveal the evolution of Muhammad's two doctrines:

1. God sent many prophets over the ages to many people groups with the same monotheistic message
2. Muhammad is the last and greatest messenger, specifically for the Arabs

Of this "perfect tablet," many non-Muslims have had a problem with its readability. For those who would attempt to read it, it's helpful to read out loud. Scholar and historian Thomas Carlyle once said of it: "It is as toilsome reading as I ever undertook, a wearisome, confused jumble, crude, incondite."[14]

Even Muslim scholar Ali Dashi remarked, "The Qor'an was badly edited and its contents are very obtusely arranged. All students of the Qor'an wonder why the editors did not use the natural and logical method of ordering by date of revelation."[15] The Koran constantly changes topics. Also, many suras appear to be dialog between people that have challenged Muhammad's revelations and what appear to be his own meditative polemic responses.

Since the time of Muhammad, many others have devised fables and claimed to not only supersede the Koran, but also the Old and New Testaments. Among them is the Baha'u'llah, the founder of the Baha'ism, who wrote *The Kitab-I-iqan*. He claimed to be the twelfth imam, the hidden Mahdi returned.

Many New Age and occult revelations could be included, but the point is that just because Muhammad received a revelation proves nothing about God's authorship of the Koran. His continuous argumentative rebuttals about the Koran being from God are more of an indictment for the opposite.

Problems with the Koran

The Koran is represented as a book that should not be doubted (Sura 2:2). It is without contradictions, according to the prophet. "Can they not consider the Koran? Were it from any other than God, they would surely have found in it many contradictions" (Sura 4:83).

There are plenty of internal problems, illogical statements, errors, and contradictions within the Koran. There are the strange verses about Allah changing people into scouted apes and swine (Sura 2:62; 5:64; 7:164) and Solomon talking with birds and ants before a host of jinn and men (Sura 27:15–19).

WITH THE BIBLE

There are discrepancies between the Koran and the Bible. This is significant because the Koran is supposedly built on the former, *valid*, God-given revelations to the Jews and Christians. In the Koran, Muhammad admonishes Muslims to respect the Book and the "people of the book." Then he changes his stance: "Fight against those who have been given the Scripture as believeth not in Allah" (Sura 9:29).

The Koran alters numerous Old Testament accounts. First, in Sura 2:93 we find that two angels named "Harut and Marut" were at the tower of Babel. However, the biblical account, Genesis 11, does not mention these angels, even though it was written 2,000 years before the Koran.

Second, numerous suras state that the angels in the Garden of Eden were ordered by Allah to prostrate themselves and worship

Adam, but Eblis (Satan) refused because of pride (Sura 7:10–21). If Allah is the only one deserving of worship, why would angels worship Adam?

Third, Muslims like to use the dubious account in Sura 37:100–110 to argue that Ishmael was to be Abraham's sacrifice.

> And when he became a full-grown youth, His father said to him, "My son, I have seen in a dream that I should sacrifice thee; therefore, consider what thou seest right." He said, "My father, do what thou art bidden; of the patient, if God please, shalt thou find me." And when they had surrendered them to the will of God, he laid him down upon his forehead: We cried unto him, "O Abraham! Now hast thou satisfied the vision." See how we recompense the righteous. This was indeed a decisive test. And we ransomed his son with a costly victim, and we left this for him among posterity, "PEACE BE ON ABRAHAM!"

Notice that no name is attached to the son in the passage, but Muslims proclaim it to be Ishmael rather than Isaac. Genesis 22 leaves no room for doubt that Isaac was the promised son of Abraham and was used to test the faithfulness of the patriarch.

WITH THE REVELATIONS

If the Koran is a repeat of what each prophet before Muhammad had received, how is it that there are specific revelations about Muhammad's own family? (For example, see Sura 33:28–33.[16]) Are we to conclude that all prior prophets received the same revelation for those around them?

Four contradictions exist in how Muhammad received the revelations.

1. Suras 53:2–18 and 81:19–24 say Allah personally appeared to Muhammad.
2. The Holy Spirit brought the Koran, according to Suras 16:102 and 26:192–194.

3. Sura 15:7–8 implies that various angels brought down the revelation.
4. Sura 2:91–92 states that only one angel, Gabriel, brought the Koran. Some Muslims downplay the contradiction by calling Gabriel the Holy Spirit (Sura 16:102), but this opens the theological prospect of the Trinity, which the Koran flatly denies.

WITH THE TRINITY

Muhammad's alleged revelation of only one God is shaky. Muhammad denies the doctrine of the Trinity in various Koranic passages (Suras 4:169 and 5:77). His misunderstanding of the doctrine was based on the concept of adding "associate gods." Still, he had already made a big mistake of adding Allah's daughters—Al-Lat, Al-Ozza, and Al-Manat—to the worship list in a move to appease his tribe. These "satanic verses" in the earliest revelation of Sura 53 nearly cost him everything. He had to reverse the revelation to retain the converts he already had.

If the Koran is perfect as God's direct revelation to Muhammad, there are *signs* that could be used to debate the theological position of the Trinity. Notice the plural form used for Allah: *Us* and *We*.

> But when our clear signs are recited to them, they who look not forward to meet Us, say, "Bring a different Koran from this, or make some change in it." (Sura 10:16)

> It is a missive from the Lord of the worlds. But if Muhammad had fabricated concerning us any sayings, We had surely seized him by the right hand, and had cut through the vein of his neck. Nor would We have withheld any one of you from him. (Sura 69:43–47)

A Christian might easily relate this to the Trinity concept shown in Genesis 1:26: "Then God said, 'Let Us make man in Our image.'"

Jihad in the Koran

In his book, *Seven Doors to Islam*, John Renard explains the orthodox views of the *greater* and *lesser* jihads. The fight within oneself is the greater struggle, and the fight against outward foes is the lesser battle. Accordingly, the lesser and greater jihad work hand-in-hand.

Islamic traditions teach that the lesser jihad fulfills the divine charge of accountability for the shape of society and the world. These "outside" battles might include human rights, environmental issues, or electing the local school board. The jihad of the sword is permitted but only as a last resort.[17] Allegedly, it should not include terrorism, mistreatment of prisoners, or the unjustifiable destruction of natural resources.

Islam divides humanity into two groups: the umma (Moslems) and the Harbi (non-Moslems).

Today, some Muslims cite verses like the following to justify their view that Islam is essentially peaceful:

> And fight for the cause of God against those who fight against you: but commit not the injustice of attacking them first: God loveth not such injustice: And kill them wherever ye shall find them, and eject them from whatever place they have ejected you; for civil discord is worse than carnage: yet attack them not at the sacred Mosque, unless they attack you therein; but if they attack you, slay them. Such is the reward of the infidels. (Sura 2:186–187)

However, history shows that Islam stormed North Africa, Europe, and Asia without being invaded first. John Kelsay explains in his book, *Islam and War: A Study in Comparative Ethics*, that seventh-century Sunni theorists saw the jihad as "the struggle to extend the boundaries of the territory of Islam." Thus, a just cause was found—or created. Lethal force was justified if non-Islamic political entities refused to pay tribute, which was the same as denying the authority of the Islamic state.[18]

Muhammad's seventh-century vision statement was Sura 2:286: "Give us victory over the infidel nations." Militant Islam has plenty of Koranic verses to back their aggressive view of the jihad. Even moderate leaders often use both aspects of the jihad's meanings to play to the crowds. "Some Muslim leaders use whatever definition suits their immediate fancy. It is not unknown for militant Arab leaders to urge foreigners to accept its [jihad] specific meaning, while gratifying followers at home by proclaiming an allegiance to the armed struggle."[19]

Below are some of the many jihad-of-the-sword verses that modern Islamic militants use to justify their actions. Note that the word *infidel* can refer to Jews, Christians, or any other "unbelievers."

URGING WAR WITH THE INFIDELS

> Infidels now are they who say, "Verily God is the Messiah Ibn Maryam (son of Mary)!" (Sura 5:19)
>
> Make war upon such of those to whom the Scriptures have been given as believe not in God [Allah]. (Sura 9:29)
>
> Believers! Wage war against such of the infidels as are your neighbors, and let them find you rigorous: and know that God is with those who fear him. (Sura 9:124)
>
> Give not way to the infidels, but by means of this Koran strive against them with a mighty strife. (Sura 25:54)

When ye encounter the infidels, strike off their heads till ye have made a great slaughter among them, and of the rest make fast the fetters. (Sura 47:4)

FORBIDDING FRIENDSHIPS WITH INFIDELS

If they turn back, then seize them, and slay them wherever ye find them; but take none of them as friends and helpers. (Sura 4:91)

Verily, the infidels are your undoubted enemies. (Sura 4:102)

O Believers! Take not the Jews or Christians as friends. They are but one another's friends. If any one of you taketh them for his friends, he surely is one of them! God will not guide the evil doers. (Sura 5:56)

Only doth God forbid you to make friends of those who on account of your religion, have warred against you, and have driven you forth from your homes, and have aided those who drove you forth: and whoever maketh friends of them are wrong doers. (Sura 60:9)

TEACHING INTOLERANCE FOR PEOPLE'S RELIGIOUS VIEWS

Kill those who join other gods to God wherever ye shall find them; and seize them, besiege them, and lay wait for them with every kind of ambush: but if they shall convert . . . then let them go their way. (Sura 9:5)

Invite not the infidels to peace when ye have the upper hand: for God is with you, and will not defraud you of the recompense of your works. (Sura 47:37)

O Prophet! Make war on the infidels and hypocrites, and deal rigorously with them. Hell shall be their abode! And wretched the passage to it! (Sura 66:9)

PROVOKING HIS MEN TO FIGHT

> But when war is commanded them, lo! A portion of them fear men as with the fear of God, or with a yet greater fear, and say: "O our Lord! Why hast thou commanded us war? Couldst thou not have given us respite till our not distant end?" Say: Small the fruition of this world; but the next life is the true good for him who feareth God! (Sura 4:79)

> What will you not fight against those Meccans who have broken their oaths and aimed to expel your Apostle, and attacked you first? Will ye dread them? God is more worthy of your fear, if ye are believers! So make war on them: By your hands will God chastise them. (Sura 9:13–14)

PROMISING ALLAH'S REWARD FOR THOSE WHO FIGHT

> Whoever fighteth on God's path, whether he be slain or conquer, we will in the end give him a great reward. (Sura 4:76)

> God hath assigned to those who contend earnestly with their persons and with their substance, a rank above those who sit at home. (Sura 4:96)

Accountability: Koran vs. Bible

Muhammad was accountable to no one for his subjective revelations. Questioning his authority might have resulted in death or military reprisal. It is sad to see that Muhammad was eventually self-deceived in his own fable and fantasy. He should have listened to his own suras:

> Let not this present life then deceive you; neither let the deceiver deceive you concerning God. (31:38)

> For the Satans will turn men aside from the Way, who yet shall deem themselves rightly guided. (43:36)

Compare the Koran's lack of accountability to the incredible amount that the Bible offers. Over 40 authors wrote the Bible during a period that covered 1600 years. Yet, the divine revelation coincides accurately and succinctly. From beginning to end, the Bible builds coherently upon a central, understandable theme.

1. God in the Garden of Eden created Adam and Eve and tested their obedience.
2. They failed, sinned, and death entered the world.
3. God, through his mercy, fashioned a plan of redemption.
4. God worked through Noah, Abraham, Isaac, Moses, David, and others to form a people—the Hebrews—who would faithfully record His Words and establish His ways in the world.
5. He promised to them the Messiah, the Great Redeemer!
6. Jesus Christ came as the Messiah, announcing that He was the Son of the Living God.
7. He referred to God as His Father.
8. His earthly mission was to teach people about the way of redemption back into the grace of God. That way was through Him and no other!
9. He proved His authority by numerous recorded miracles.
10. He then died on the cross for people's sins and rose again from the dead on the third day, thus fulfilling the many prophecies about him in the Old Testament.
11. After instructing His disciples, He ascended into heaven before many witnesses. He will return for all those who place their faith and trust in Him alone for salvation.

The Bible begins with the account of a garden and men, and it ends with the redemption of men standing before God in His garden.

The Bible obviously impressed Muhammad. Major portions of the Koran are simply supportive statements about the lives of biblical characters and many of their deeds. However, Muhammad often alters events and the presentation of biblical individuals to his own distorted worldview. To him, Jesus could not be God or the Son of God, because that would mess up Muhammad's theological philosophy and his own personal claim to be the seal of the prophets—the greatest and last.

PART FOUR

WRESTLING AGAINST PRINCIPALITIES AND POWERS

CHAPTER 9

NAME ABOVE ALL NAMES

Setting: Baghdad, 8th century.

"You're locking me up for my *scholarly* views on the Koran?"

"Thank the Hadith people," said the jailer. "They found favor with Harun al-Rashid, and it seems you lost it. Personally, they should have locked you up a long time ago."

Wasan grabbed the bars of his cell. "Why, what did I do?"

Zayd was wary. He did not like this kind. They shook up the status quo and acted so smart. "Well, for one thing you and that whole lot of Mu'tazilites are heretics, saying that the Koran is not from Allah—"

"What are you talking about? Of course, the Koran is from Allah. Get it right, man! I just don't think it is the uncreated Word of God."

The jailer was unimpressed. "Don't give me any of your fancy doubletalk. I heard you say to the judge that 'the Koran is not the perfect eternal tablet come down from heaven.'"

"Do you think the Koran is eternal and uncreated, just like Allah?"

"Of course!" snorted Zayd. "If you had any common sense, you would too."

Wasan was too tired to argue. It had been a long day. "Believe what you want." Then he turned to the small bed and stretched out with a sigh.

Zayd was perplexed. Had he beaten the scholar at his own game? Win or lose, a good conversation was far better than another boring evening in the jail office. In a conciliatory tone, he plowed on. "Well, Wasan, I actually figured you had an answer for me. Why do you think the way you do?"

Wasan closed his eyes and said, "Okay, Zayd. Let me ask you a question. If Allah and the Koran are both uncreated, then which is greater?"

Zayd started to answer and then bit his lip. Content with his mental calculations, he said, "Allah, of course."

"Allah could only be greater if Allah *created* the Koran. If the Koran existed forever along with Allah, then it is equal to Allah himself." Zayd mulled this over. It was interesting—and dangerous. Wasan kept up the pressure. "Consider the concept of the Koran as the Word of God. Do you know that the Christians called Jesus the Word of God?" Zayd did not, but Wasan didn't wait for an answer. "In fact, the Prophet Muhammad himself said that Jesus was the Word of God. Look for yourself in the fourth sura. The Koran must be the *words* of Allah, which cannot be equal to Allah himself. Think about it. When you hold the Koran, are you holding Allah? If no one has ever seen Allah, how can the Koran be him? When it is read, are you hearing

Muslims claim the lineage of Ishmael, the son born to Abraham by Hagar.

Allah in person? And what about Jesus? If he is the Word, then is he really Allah, like the Christians say. If not, is he the Koran?"

Zayd was swimming in the flood of new ideas. Like most Sunni, he had been content to simply accept the Koran as the eternal tablet and dismiss the contradictions. "Yes, . . . well, those certainly are deep questions. I have to go and see if any other prisoners have arrived." He spun and started off with long strides.

Wasan had more. "But Zayd, we're not done with the choice of free will."

"Ah, not now. The streets of Baghdad are full of thieves, you know."

Closing his eyes again, Wasan knew he had time on his side.

Although issues about the Koran's validity have been discussed, it should be noted that some of the text is based firmly in truth. For instance, the miracles Jesus performed are listed accurately. Interestingly, God has used these elements of truth to reveal Himself to those who do not have access to the Bible. An amazing testimony of a Muslim girl who converted to Christianity is found in the life of Gulshan Esther. Her story, told in *The Torn Veil*, takes place in Punjab, Pakistan, in the 1960s and 1970s. She was the youngest daughter of a Shiite Muslim Sayed family that descended directly from the prophet Muhammad.

At six months of age, Gulshan contracted typhoid and became completely paralyzed in half of her body. Soon afterward, her mother died. Gulshan's siblings and relatives lovingly cared for her, especially her father, who never remarried. He prayed for her healing constantly. They traveled to London to find the best doctors, and went on a hajj to Mecca to kiss the Black Stone and ask Allah for healing. Nothing worked.

When Gulshan was a teenager, her father died. Gulshan was heartsick at the loss—and now a lonely, crippled orphan. The prayer beads and the Koran that had been important in the past didn't bring her peace. God seemed distant. She despised being a burden to others. The emotional pain grew until suicide became a easy choice, but then she lacked the mobility or means to do so. Tears flowed, and for the first time in her life she asked God openly for help. Amazed, she heard, "I am Jesus, son of Mary. Read about me in the Koran."

Gulshan conversed with Jesus and read about Him in the Koran. Several years later, she cried again. This time, it was for the Jesus of the Koran to heal her. In a vision, Jesus commanded her to get up and walk.

She did.

He said, "I am Jesus. I am Immanuel. I am the Way, the Truth, and Life. I am alive, and I am soon coming. See, from today you are my witness."[1] Then He taught her the Lord's Prayer.

I met a couple who heard Gulshan speak years ago in Mississauga, Canada. They were surprised to notice that one of her fingers was still crippled. Why hadn't it been healed with the rest? Apparently, Jesus left her with one crippled finger to continuously remind her of the divine healing in her life.

Gulshan's story exploded in the community, and she gave all the glory to Jesus. Eventually, people pressured her to stop talking so much about Jesus, but she could not. She was a missionary for the Lord.

Jesus Christ: Healer and Miracle Worker

What did Gulshan learn about Jesus in the Koran? In the Arabic Koran, Jesus (*Isa*) is referred to over thirty times. Readers are introduced to a more limited and distorted Jesus than the one in the Bible, but that is due to the setting in which it was written.[2] Muhammad's information of Jesus was restricted. There was no Arabic translation of the Bible, so accurate biblical information was hard to come by, especially in those days before the printing press. Apparently, Waraqa ibn-Nawfal, the cousin of Muhammad's wife Khadijah, was a Christian and might have recited the oral traditions that he had heard from the incomplete version of the Bible that existed in the Syriac language.

In those days, only clerics and monks had a scholarly knowledge of Christianity. Thus, many of the Christian Arabs were not well versed in orthodoxy. They swayed in their views toward the Monophysites or Nestorians. The Monophysites leaned heavily on Christ's divinity but at the expense of His humanity.

The Nestorians were a reaction to the Monophysites. They held that within the incarnate Christ were two separate persons: one divine, one human.[3] His perfect obedience overcame the devil, and his perfect service was a role model of humility for all mankind to follow.

One other group of Christians may have influenced Muhammad's writing of the Koran. Theologian Hans Küng has suggested that a small group of Messianic Jews existed in Mecca, although they did not regard Jesus as divine.[4]

The Koran doesn't say much about the attributes of Jesus. It says enough for those who are searching—genuinely probing—for the truth to see that Jesus Christ was unlike any other man who ever lived, including Muhammad. Consider the following suras:

> . . . to Jesus, son of Mary, gave we clear proofs of his mission, and strengthened him by the Holy Spirit. (Sura 2:81)

> Out of clay will I [Isa] make for you, as it were, the figure of a bird: and I will breath into it, and it shall become, by God's leave,

> a bird. And I will heal the blind, and the leper; and by God's leave will I quicken the dead. (Sura 3:43)
>
> And she made a sign to them, pointing toward the babe. They said, "How shall we speak with him who is in the cradle, an infant?" It [Isa] said, "Verily, I am the servant of God; He [Allah] hath given me the Book, and He hath made me a prophet." (Sura 19:30–31)
>
> And when the Son of Mary was set forth as an instance of divine power, lo! Thy people cried out for joy thereat. (Sura 43:57)

In these verses, we see that Jesus had a specific mission. He was strengthened by the Holy Spirit and displayed divine power. Five special miracles are here recorded as examples of His divine power:

1. Heal the blind
2. Heal the lepers
3. Quicken (raise) the dead
4. Create a bird from clay and breath life into it
5. Speak from the cradle as a babe

The first three miracles are validated in the Bible. The fourth and fifth are not. It is unlikely that He spoke from the cradle. Whether Jesus actually created the bird is debatable, but the information about it probably came to Muhammad through an apocryphal book entitled the Gospel of Thomas.[5] It is interesting that the bird miracle could be said to resemble the Genesis account of God creating man and breathing life into him (Gen. 2:7).

The other three miracles help define the greatness of Jesus divine power. No healing was impossible; even the dead were raised. The Christian New Testament records numerous eye-witness accounts of miracles, including stopping the wind and waves, feeding 5,000 from a few fishes and loaves of bread, casting out demons, walking on water, and turning water into wine. As mentioned in the Koran, these produced great joy in the people.

Sura 42:11 speaks of having faith. For Christians, this means having a firm trust and belief in Him for everything. Sura 33:7 tells of the covenant that Allah made with Isa. For followers of Isa, this is the New Covenant, New Testament, or Injil.

Jesus Christ: Sign from God

> Some of the apostles we have endowed more highly than others: Those to whom God hath spoken, He hath raised to the loftiest grade, and to Jesus the Son of Mary we gave manifest signs, and we strengthened him with Holy Spirit. (Sura 2:254)

> And make mention in the Book of Mary, when she went apart from her family eastward, and took a veil to shroud herself from them: and we sent our spirit to her, and he took before her the form of a perfect man. She said, "I fly for refuge from thee to the God of Mercy! If thou fearest Him, begone from me." He said: "I am only a messenger of thy Lord, that I may bestow on thee a holy son." She said: "How shall I have a son, when man hath never touched me? And I am not unchaste." He said: "So shall it be. Thy Lord hath said: 'Easy is this with me;' and we will make him a sign to mankind, and a mercy from us. For it is a thing decreed." And she conceived him. (Sura 19:16–22)

> We breathed our spirit, and made her and her son a sign to all creatures. (Sura 21:91)

> And we appointed the Son of Mary, and His mother for a sign. (Sura 23:52)

Part of Jesus' divine mission was to be a sign. Allah sent His *spirit* and created a holy son as a sign for mankind. When Christians read this, it reminds us of Luke 1, where the angel Gabriel announces to Mary that she would conceive a Son named Jesus, "the Son of the Highest" (Luke 1:32). Mary did not understand how she, as a virgin, could have a child.

> And the angel answered and said to her, "The Holy Spirit will come upon you, and the power of the Highest will overshadow you; therefore, also, that Holy One who is to be born will be called the Son of God." (Injil, Luke 1:35)

The event took place and was recorded six hundred years prior to Muhammad. So, for Christians, the matter is simple—Jesus was birthed by the Holy Spirit through the Virgin Mary and is the Holy One, the Son of God. However, in the Koran, Jesus is presented as the son of Mary and not as the Son of God. To Muslims, it is blasphemy to associate Allah's divine nature with human nature. Jesus, then, can only be a created being. In Sura 3, He is compared to Adam as one of the only two prophets born without natural fathers.[6]

Once again, there are textual problems with the Koran. Gabriel fills the position of the Holy Spirit and is a part of the "we" that refers to Allah. The angel is represented as a perfect man. His answer that he may bestow on Mary a holy son raises the question whether or not that was to be accomplished through carnal action. In reality, the virgin birth was prophesied and recorded long before the time of Mary by the prophet Isaiah, who also referred to the Son's divinity:

> Therefore the Lord Himself will give you a sign: Behold, the virgin shall conceive and bear a Son, and shall call His name Immanuel (meaning God with us). (Suhuf-un Nabiyin, Isaiah 7:14)

In 1947, a wandering Bedouin goat herdsman explored a cave in the side of the cliffs west of the Dead Sea. He found approximately 40,000 fragments of papyrus from Old Testament books and other ancient literature. It was called the greatest archeological discovery of the twentieth century. A complete book of Isaiah was found that dates to at least 125 BC. It was recorded from earlier manuscripts of the same book. The authenticity is beyond dispute. It bears witness to the sign of the virgin bearing a Son who would be God with us.[7] Furthermore, Isaiah prophesies about the unique divine attributes of Jesus that were not portrayed in the Koran. Jesus has a name that cannot be matched by any other:

> For unto us a Child is born, unto to us a Son is given; and the government will be upon His shoulder: And His name will be called Wonderful, Counselor, Mighty God, Everlasting Father, Prince of Peace. Of the increase of his government and peace there will be no end. Upon the throne of David and over His kingdom, to order it and establish it with judgment and justice from that time forward, even forever. The zeal of the Lord of hosts will perform this. (Isaiah 9:6–7)

Jesus Christ: Messiah

> Remember when the angel said, "O Mary! Verily God announceth to thee the Word from Him: His name shall be, Messiah Jesus the son of Mary, illustrious in this world, and in the next, and one of those who have near access to God; and He shall speak to men alike when in the cradle and when grown up; and he shall be one of the just." (Sura 3:40–41)

The Koran ascribes the title of Messiah to Jesus eleven times, but it never defines it. The word *messiah* in Hebrew means "the anointed one." *Christ* is the Greek equivalent in place of Messiah. So *Messiah Jesus* and *Christ Jesus* are similar. Jesus never used the word *Christ* to refer to himself, but He commended Peter for recognizing it (Matthew 16:16–17), and he admitted to being the Christ at his trial (26:63–64).[8]

For Muhammad, Jesus was an apostle but not the Savior. For Christians and many Jews, the Messiah is the Savior of mankind.

The Greek name *Jesus* or its Hebrew equivalent, *Yeshua*, mean "savior." The angel told Joseph that Jesus was given that name because He would "save His people from their sins" (Matthew 1:21). John the Baptist said of Jesus, "Behold, the Lamb who takes away the sins of the world" (John 1:29).

Jesus Christ: Word of God

> The Messiah, Jesus, son of Mary, is only an apostle of God, and his Word which he conveyed into Mary, and a Spirit proceeding from himself. (Sura 4:169)

This bit of truth in the Koran confirms a major biblical revelation. Jesus came as the living Word of God. It is also amazing that Jesus is represented as Allah's Spirit. Jesus, then, is Allah's Word and Allah's Spirit. As seen earlier, He is also Messiah. No other prophet in the Koran has this description, not even Muhammad!

This is not denying the Koranic exhortation that there is only one God. Christians agree. Injil, Mark 12:32 proclaims, "There is one God, and there is no other but He." The central teaching of Christianity is that Jesus Christ is God! The orthodox doctrine of the Trinity coincides with this. When Muslims truly understand what Christians mean by the Trinity, they realize that Christians also believe in one God.

The doctrine of the Trinity states that within the nature of the one God there are three eternal persons:

- God the Father
- God the Son
- God the Holy Spirit

Jesus sent His disciples to all nations and told them to make disciples and baptize "in the name of the Father and of the Son and of the Holy Spirit" (Injil, Matthew 28:19). Jesus is the Creator of all that is; He is not the created. He defined Himself in the Word of God.

In his book *Al-Masih: The Anointed One*, author and Muslim outreach expert Noor ul Haq explains:

> As Word of Allah (kalimatullah), Al-Masih Isa was the direct revelation of Allah's will for mankind. In the days of the ancient prophets, Allah revealed His will through the Word of the Holy Books. Now He had revealed His will through the Word of a living human being named Al-Masih Isa.[9]

> In the beginning was the Word, and the Word was with God, and the Word was God. (Injil, John 1:1)

> And the Word became flesh and dwelt among us, and we beheld His glory, the glory as of the only begotten of the Father, full of grace and truth. (Injil, John 1:14)

> He was clothed with a robe dipped in blood, and His name is called the Word of God. (Injil, Revelation 19:13)

It is interesting that Muslims believe each verse of the Koran as a written sign. The Word of God—the Messiah Jesus—came as the incomparable sign of God and revealed God in the flesh. Muslims believe that the Koran is the perfect tablet that came down from heaven. In truth, Jesus Christ is the perfect tablet that came down from heaven, as revealed in the Bible. Interestingly, God did not speak every word that was recorded in the Bible, as Muslims believe of the Koran. Some of the words are transcripts of conversations of men or demons; others are lists of

Islamic law equates the testimony of two women to one man.

historical facts. Still, all of the text is consistent and unified in its purpose to reveal God's message of love and salvation.

Author David Hubbard says it well in his book, *Does the Bible Really Work?*

> It says exactly what God wants it to say, and every part of it is important. But one thing more needs to be said, briefly, the Bible is the Word of God. In other words, the Bible's inspiration is permanent, part of its very nature. It does not depend on how we feel about it. The Bible's inspiration is not its ability to turn me on but the fact that God has breathed His own truth in all its sentences and words.[10]

Jesus Christ: Merciful One

> She said: "How shall I have a son, when man hath never touched me? And I am not unchaste." He said: "So shall it be. Thy Lord hath said: 'Easy is this with me;' and we will make him a sign to mankind, and a mercy from us. For it is a thing decreed." And she conceived him. (Sura 19:20–22)

> We caused Jesus the son of Mary to follow them; and we gave him the Evangel [gospel], and we put into the hearts of those who followed him kindness and compassion. (Sura 57:27)

Here, motive is added to the mission of Jesus: "a mercy from us [Allah]." Author Noor ul Haq, in his thoughtful booklet entitled *Mercy of Allah*, says that Jesus "was the outstretched hand of Allah. He was the living expression and the personification of Allah's redeeming Mercy."[11] It is interesting that of the 99 names that the Koran has for Allah, *al-Rahman* (Allah, the Merciful, the Compassionate) is found 169 times. Al-Rahman was one of the popular monotheistic deities in southern Arabia whose attribute was adopted for Allah by Muhammad and incorporated into the Koran.

The Koran presents Jesus as a sign of God's mercy and compassion. He was given the Evangel, which was His teaching of the gospel, the good news of the New Testament. Here is the basic gospel message:

> For God so loved the world that He gave His only begotten Son, that whoever believes in Him should not perish but have everlasting life. (John 3:16)

> Moreover brethren, I declare to you the gospel . . . that Christ died for our sins according to the Scriptures, and that He was buried, and that He rose again the third day according to the Scriptures. (Injil, 1 Corinthians 15:1–4)

God the Father loved people so much that He sent His Son, Jesus Christ, to be the Savior of mankind by dying on the cross for our sins. Isaiah prophesied that Jesus would bear "the sin of many" (Isaiah 53:12), but he also said that Jesus would bear our grief, sorrows, transgressions, and that "by His stripes we are healed" (53:4–5). Those who accept the sacrifice of Al-Masih Isa on their behalf and place their faith in Him will not perish but have everlasting life.

Jesus Christ: Risen Savior

Jesus did not stay in the grave but rose on the third day. Sura 19:34 mentions Jesus being "raised to life," but it does not say when it happened. Of course, Muslims are not taught that Jesus died on the cross; therefore, the resurrection is a moot point.

The following passage has produced much diversity of thought within Islam:

> And for their saying, "Verily, we have slain the Messiah, Jesus the son of Mary, an Apostle of God." Yet they slew him not and they crucified him not, but they had only his likeness. (Sura 4:156)

The crucifixion of Al-Masih Isa is one of the most well documented facts in history.[12] Muhammad was either misinformed, misunderstood, or had ulterior motives. Either way, it sets up Muslim scholars with a real dilemma. Some have tried to explain it away by saying Jesus hid while one of his companions died in His place. Others believe that God sent angels to protect Jesus, and Judas Iscariot died in His place. Another tradition says God took Jesus to heaven before the Jews could kill Him.[13]

A Muslim scholar named Mahmoud M. Ayoub suggests Muhammad was misunderstood. It is his position that the Koran "does not deny the death of Christ. Rather, it challenges human beings who in their folly delude themselves into believing that they would vanquish the divine Word, Jesus Christ the Messenger of God."[14] Another author, Harry Morin, agrees with Ayoub's assessment that the Koran does not deny the crucifixion and death of Jesus, "Most Muslims accept the birth of Jesus and the raising of Jesus into heaven. It should not be so difficult then for them to believe that somewhere in between, Jesus died."[15]

Finally, Muhammad may have denied the crucifixion because he feared receiving a similar treatment if things got out of hand. So he revealed that the Christians and Jews were mistaken. Muhammad did not want to suffer. He did not come to be a savior, and he could not imagine that God would become a man and suffer for others. Yet, as John Stott points out, that is why the suffering on the cross implies that Jesus is God:

> I could never myself believe in God, if it was not for the Cross. In the real world of pain, how could one worship a God who was immune to it? I have entered many Buddhist temples in different Asian countries and stood respectfully before the statue of the Buddha, his legs crossed, arms folded, eyes closed, the ghost of a smile playing round his mouth, a remote look on his face, detached from the agonies of the world. But each time, after a while I have had to turn away. And in imagination I have turned instead to that lonely, twisted, tortured figure on the cross, nails through hands and feet, back lacerated, limbs wretched, brow

> bleeding from throne pricks, mouth dry and intolerably thirsty, plunged in God-forsaken darkness. That is the God for me! He laid aside his immunity to pain. He entered our world of flesh and blood, tears and death. He suffered for us. Our sufferings become more manageable in the light of his. There is still a question mark against human suffering, but over it we boldly stamp another mark, the Cross, which symbolizes divine suffering.[16]

Jesus Christ: Name Above All Names

> And being found in appearance as a man, He humbled Himself and became obedient to the point of death, even the death of the cross. Therefore God also has highly exalted Him and given Him the name which is above every name, that at the name of Jesus every knee should bow, of those in heaven, and of those on earth, and of those under the earth, and that every tongue should confess that Jesus Christ is Lord, to the glory of God the Father. (Injil, Philippians 2:8–11)

Muslims reject the Trinity and believe that Christians worship three gods.

Jesus (Isa) delivered a crushing blow to Satan (Shaitan) and the demonic jinn when He rose from the dead. The process will eventually end with the destruction of Shaitan and his cohorts. Death itself will be cast into the lake of fire. Because Jesus endured the shame of the cross, He has now become the author and finisher of people's faith. The Holy Scripture teaches that there is salvation in no other name accept for Jesus Christ. Eventually, every knee will bow to Him and confess Him as Lord (Injil, Hebrews 2:14; 4:10, 12; 12:2. Injil, Revelation 20:10; 21:8).

Shaitan and the jinn are not yet thrown in the lake of fire. The Apostle Paul wrote that Shaitan is trying to blind men's minds to the triumph of Jesus Christ. In the last days people will turn from the faith and give heed to deceiving jinn and their doctrines. Before Al-Masih Isa returns, there will be great deception, hatred, and lawlessness; false prophets will deceive many; nations and kingdoms will war against one another; and there will be famines, pestilences, and earthquakes. His gospel will be preached as a witness to every nation, and then the end will come (Injil, Matthew 24:4–14; Corinthians 4:4; 1 Timothy 4:1).

There are great battles between the Kingdom of God and the forces of darkness:

> Finally, my brethren, be strong in the Lord and in the power of His might. Put on the whole armor of God, that you may be able to stand against the wiles of the devil. For we do not wrestle against flesh and blood, but against principalities, against powers, against the rulers of the darkness of this age, against spiritual host of wickedness in the heavenly places. (Injil, Ephesians 6:10–12)

The warfare is spiritual, waged by Christians against the satanic principalities and rulers of the world who attack the lives of people who are without Christ. Spiritual armor is necessary for the spiritual warrior, and the most powerful weapon is prayer. [17]

CHAPTER 10

ALLAH WEEPS

Setting: The country of Sudan, late 1990s.

Ayesha searched the faces of the crowd that gathered around the base of the auction block. None reflected hope. It seemed only suffering had followed her since she was taken from her home in the spring. Ayesha remembered it easily. The weather had been agreeable that morning. Her father and brother had just returned from the mosque as she and her sisters were heading for the market.

Truck engines and machine guns shattered the peaceful afternoon. Fear was everywhere, and she quickly sought cover for her sisters. The littler girls fit nicely under a blanket, camouflaged in a vendor's shop, but she was too big. Ayesha ran across the street to seek more shelter but didn't make it. The spotter saw her, and she was soon among the captives. Then the nightmare unfolded over months of confinement, toilsome tasks, and the groping hands of the National Islamic Front guards.

But now, would Allah answer her prayers? Her eyes darted, searching for liberation in the crowd, a friendly face. She was far from her village but knew that sometimes parents showed up to purchase their own children. No one was in the crowd. Still, she had heard stories of wealthy Christian foreigners who bought slaves and gave them freedom. The Swiss-based Christian Solidarity International had gained a heroic reputation in the last few years.

If only Mom and Dad could see her now, being leered at by men. She fought back the tears as the auctioneer made her walk around the platform to show off her young form. "Three dollars, now four, is the bid. Do I here five, six, seven? What about ten?" The bidding had reached eighteen dollars but was slowing.

A poor farmer hobbled up to the auctioneer, leading a cow, and said, "I'll bid a cow and one dollar. I have three cows but no one to give me pleasure." The man's slow gait exposed his age and sickness.

The bidding stopped momentarily while the auctioneer examined the animal. When satisfied, he continued, "The bid is a cow and one dollar. Any other bids?"

Ayesha eyed the farmer out of the corner of her eye, too afraid to catch his gaze. She could tell his teeth were missing, and the grime of his skin must have been there for weeks. Surely, this would not be her future. One last hope. One last prayer. "Allah, help me. . . ."

The auctioneer was satisfied. He clapped his hands and said, "Sold to this lucky farmer for one dollar and this cow."

Hassan grew up in an Islamic fundamentalist country. He hated seeing crosses around the necks of his Christian schoolmates. Up until he was a young adult, those children continued to feel his wrath with zealous verbal abuse, belittlement in any activity, and physical attacks.

One night, Hassan dreamed he was wearing his own cross and Muslims were ridiculing him about it. He finally understood a small portion of what Jesus had suffered on the cross. His zeal for persecuting Christians became a zeal for learning about Christ. He located a missionary, got a Bible, and began clarifying his thoughts by writing them down. Six months later, his mother discovered his writings and his father had Hassan arrested.

Today, Hassan lives in another country but stays in contact with his family and prays for them. He continues to witness about the peace and truth found in Al-Masih Isa.[1]

Many Muslems are forbidden to even say the word *pork*.

By reading the Bible, Hassan discovered that Al-Masih Isa wept over Jerusalem. Jesus knew the Jews would reject the peace and truth found only in Him, and He knew the city would be destroyed as a result (Injil, Luke 19:41–44). Similarly, Allah must be heartbroken over the warring Islamic spirit that incurs great harm in His name. He must weep for Muslims who forsake the peace and truth found only in Al-Masih Isa.

For those who might think that there is little hope for peace in the Middle East, consider the story of Walid. Like most Muslims, he was taught to hate the Jews. Raised in Bethlehem and Jericho in the 1960s in a Muslim home, Walid saw the conflict and wars between Jews and Muslims up close. The first song he learned in school was "Arabs Our Beloved and Jews Our Dogs." As a teen, he promoted the intifada by rioting and throwing Molotov cocktails at the Israeli army. Walid said he was angry at Hitler because he didn't finish the job of eradicating the Jews.

Walid' mother was American but his father a Palestinian teacher of English and Islamic Studies. After moving to the U.S. for a college education, Walid's mother converted to Christianity and witnessed of the Bible's accuracy. Walid read a Christian book on the End Times and became intrigued about Jesus. In his comparisons of the Bible to the Koran, he used the Dead Sea Scrolls to help him conclude that the Bible was accurate and the Koran was not. Finally, Walid prayed for revelation and came to know Jesus Christ. It amazed him that this same Jesus was a *Jew* from Bethlehem. The name *Bethlehem* means "home of the bread." Walid recognized Jesus as the Bread of Life and the one who came to give life to all, including Muslims and Jews.

Today, Walid proclaims love for the Jews and says he weeps for them and is ready to give his "own life for them, as did my Lord." Quite a change.

Islam, Judaism, and Christianity: The Differences

Secular writers, sociologists, and historians may look thoughtfully at the outward appearance of Islam, Christianity, and Judaism, but unless they get to the "spirit" of the matter they will miss

RELIGION	SCRIPTURE	PERMISSION TO USE ARMS	CONQUEST AND GOAL
Islam	Koran	Yes	Global domination
Judaism	Old Testament	Yes	Israel and its territories
Christianity	New Testament (and OT)	No	Global evangelization

out on the spiritual forces behind these religions. For instance, in comparing the spiritual worldview of these three, which includes written directives for arms and struggle for the advancement of their religion?

Islam: Muhammad killed men. He preached and lived the Jihad. His successors, the caliphs, took up coercion and swords to extend Islam to all the neighboring nations. The Koran embraces the violence, arms, and coercion that modern Muslims use to justify the spread of its message to the entire world. Verses used to defend the Koran as a book of peace are easily countered by other, fundamentalist verses. Allowing warfare to continue unchecked is a breeding ground for demonic activity.

Judaism: Moses killed an Egyptian when he was young. Later, God used him to miraculously lead the Hebrews out of Egypt and through the wilderness. This included warfare against imposing nations—Canaanites, Philistines, and others—to conquer the lands that were promised by God. Deuteronomy 30:3–6 speaks prophetically of the Jews regaining Israel. The Old Testament embraces but limits the aggressiveness of Jews to the defense or capture of their territories.

Christianity: Jesus lived a life of perfect peace, truth, and love. He taught that the greatest commandment was to love God and others. He miraculously ministered to other people's needs, even to die on the cross for anyone who will receive His offer of eternal life. He was the ultimate picture of selflessness and sacrifice. After He rose from the dead, He commissioned his disciples to live the same way and take the gospel message into the entire world. Of those disciples Jesus commissioned, all but John the Apostle was martyred in foreign lands while peacefully preaching the good news.[2] The New Testament does not embrace violence, arms, or coercion to spread its message. Any use of those by modern Christians to spread their faith is strictly their own doing.

Violence and Christianity

The Koran is a document that binds the minds and hearts of Muslims, thwarting even their best efforts for peace. The limited moral fiber in the book has chained social fairness, immobilized the quest for truth, and unleashed a relentless sword.

Secular commentators have tried to include Christianity in the same category. Certainly, some actions by rogue Christians have been deplorable, justifying violence by taking verses from the Old Testament out of context and reapplying them to support their own agendas. That was not Christ's example. He embraced the Old Testament as a model for inner spiritual principles and truths, not outward physical violence. Nowhere in the New Testament does He command his people to wipe out other nations. On the contrary, Jesus told us to love our enemies (Matthew 5:44). The word *love* appears in the New Testament over 175 times.

It is a mistake to say that Jesus supported violence because of his statements about the sword in Matthew 10:34 and Luke 22:36, where He asserts that He came to bring a sword and not peace, or tells His disciples to sell their garments and buy a sword. Once again, in context with the rest of Jesus' words and actions, and those of all the New Testament authors, those statements have proven to be symbolic. In fact, when facing Roman soldiers who had orders to take him by force, Jesus healed the man whose ear had been cut off by Peter. Then He reprimanded Peter for the act of violence, "All who take the sword shall perish by the sword" (Matthew 26:52). The Apostle Paul explains the symbolism of the Christian sword as the Bible, the Word of God (Ephesians 6:17), which can divide the soul and spirit (Hebrews 4:12).

What about Christians in the armed forces? Christian men and women go to battle to defend their country and to protect their families, not to spread their religion. The Bible can be used to justify conscientious objectors, who are morally opposed to fighting, or it can be used to affirm one's responsibility to obey the governing authorities (Romans 13). Clearly, there is no recognizable fundamentalist Christian military marching with orders from the New Testament to ensure people turn to Jesus or die.

Did Christians use weapons during the Crusades to propagate their faith? Yes, they did—and they were wrong to try to spread Christianity in that manner. Fortunately, that kind of campaign would not happen now. Consider a few issues of the time period:

- Few people owned Bibles
- Most Bibles were in ancient language that no one but scholars could read
- Church services were liturgical and in a language only the elite understood
- The Pope was erroneously considered to be God's voice and supreme authority in the world

Today, the Bible is available to the common man, is preached in modern languages, and most Christians realize that the Pope and other religious leaders are quite fallible. The Bible is the ultimate authority in matters of faith, not a religious leader who has political goals.

What about the Catholic-Protestant conflict in Ireland? The Christian world agrees that the fighting between Catholics and Protestants should stop permanently. They should live in peace according to the admonition of the New Testament. Still, to clarify further, the fighting in Ireland is being carried out by secular, politicized mobs that are using Christianity as an attack vehicle. They employ Old Testament contention, rather than justifying their actions through the New Testament. In addition, it's *within* Christendom, so to speak. They are not trying to bring Christian law to the world through violence, as is the strategy of Islamic militants with Shariah Law.

What about fanatical cults? It's easy to find fanatics who abuse religion. In 1977, Jim Jones in Jonestown, Guyana, thinking he had been reincarnated as Buddha, Jesus, and others, lead 914 people into suicide or had them murdered.[3] In 1995, Shoko Asahara, leader of a Buddhist apocalyptic cult, Aum Shinri Kyo, was responsible for a nerve gas bomb in a Japanese subway station that killed 12 and hospitalized 5,000.[4] Of course, there are also ultra-conservative Christians who have killed abortionists in the name of God. There are White Supremacists who erroneously consider themselves Christians as they continue to terrorize and kill people out of racial bigotry. Any reasonable study of their doctrine uncovers a consistent fondness for twisting the Bible, or whatever religious book they employ.

A common White Supremacist doctrine is called the *serpent seed doctrine*. This dangerous invention says that Eve had sex with Satan, producing Cain. Later, Satan had sex with Rebekah (Isaac's wife), producing Esau. Then the claim is that from Esau came all the darker races, a people who do not have souls. This deranged doctrine is clearly a distortion of the Old Testament.

Interestingly, the bogus doctrine of the Supremacists can be easily compared to that of the Alawite branch of modern Islam, a branch that is contrary to mainstream Islam. These adherents believe that women do not have souls. Syria's president, Bashar al-Assad, embraces it.[5] The Koran implies that women are worth less then men. Males receive twice the inheritance of females (Sura 4:12). Also, under Shariah Law, it takes two women to equal the voice of one man in a dispute.[6] So, although the Alawite position on women is not popular within Islam, the doctrine is easily justified and understood after a simple reading of the Koran or Hadith. Even so, mainstream Muslims do not embrace this erratic doctrine.

All religions have extremes, but the true warring spirit of the Koran is not held in check by Islam extremists and is rarely condemned by mainstream Islam.

Exporting Islam Worldwide

In the 1980s the Universal Islamic Declaration of the Islamic Council of Europe was created. Article VI, entitled the "Liberation of Muslim Lands," states:

> The subjugation of Muslim people and the occupation of their lands in certain parts of the world is matter of grave concern to us. The most painful of these is the usurpation and occupation of the holy city of Jerusalem (al-Quds). It is the sacred duty of umma to mobilize itself fully and strive relentlessly to liberate Jerusalem and all other Muslim lands.[7]

In April of 1989, on the Khyber Pass between Afghanistan and Pakistan, a group came together at a training camp to learn warfare and help the Mujahideen to fight the Russians. The Muslim camp was training Filipino Moros; Uzbeks from Soviet Central Asia; Arabs from Algeria, Egypt, Saudi Arabia, and Kuwait; and Uighurs from Xinjiang in China. One evening, a journalist asked Lieutenant General Hameed Gul, the head of the Pakistani Interservices Intelligence (ISI) whether or not he was playing with fire by inviting all these radicals who could potentially cause dissension in their own countries. General Gul answered, "We are fighting the jihad and this is the first Islamic international brigade in the modern era. The communists have their international brigades, the West has NATO, why can't the Muslims unite and form a common front?"[8] Eventually, the many training camps would have direct influence over 100,000 Muslim radicals who were training for jihad.[9]

Sudan got involved in terrorism in 1991, when the Popular International Organization (PIO) held a conference for terrorist organizations from over fifty-five countries. This was a Sunni revolutionary group whose objective was a global action plan against the West because Allah could no longer remain in the world.[10]

On January 2, 1992, Ahmad Khomeini, son of the late Ayatollah Khomeini, embraced the tenets of his father by proposing this vision statement for modern Islamic fundamentalism:

> Iran's Islamic revolution has awakened all the Islamic countries. . . . Islam recognizes no borders. We cannot put off establishing Islamic governments and administrating the divine laws. The objective of the Islamic Republic and its officials is none other than to establish a global Islamic rule. . . . Political means may differ, but no revolutionary Muslim ever forgets the objective.[11]

During the Ayatollah Khomeini's regime and shortly afterward, there were forty-nine accounts of terrorist's activities against Iranian exiles, including in Europe and the United States.[12] Within Iran, there were more than 100,000 executions of Mujahideen, the principle force that opposed the fundamentalism of Khomeini and his son and sought for democracy and the equality of women.

On May 23, 1997, the moderate Khatami was elected in Iran. Hope spawned when he made positive overtures to the West by overturning the Khomeini fatwah to assassinate author Salman Rushdie for writing *The Satanic Verses*.[13] The book portrays Muhammad as one who has been deceived by Satan, or as one who made up the stories to deceive others. Yet, Iran still didn't change. In April of 1998, Ayatollah Khamenei ordered an international terror campaign against the United States and Israel. The focus for terror was to promote Islamic revival.[14]

The Palestinian Hamas created a rationale along these lines. In their charter, they justified the present *al-intifitada* (the shaking off of illegitimate rule) against Israel by citing the Crusades as a military move that was basically an ideological attack. [15] The Islamic Jihad of Egypt used the same reasoning to assassinate Anwar Sadat. Their "testament," called *The Neglected Duty*, defines their modern justification for attacking the West and Israel and attempts to throw off all non-Islamic authority.[16]

In his book *America and Third World War*, Osama bin Laden calls all Muslims to a global jihad against the United States. He holds up the Koran and says, "You cannot defeat heretics with this book alone; you have to show them the fist."

Bin Laden's Islamic Front was made up of former Afghan Mujahideen, including Egyptians, Jordanians, Palestinians, Lebanese, Algerians, Pakistanis, and even Americans.[17] His al-Qaeda terrorist network reaches across five continents and dozens of countries, incorporating a clandestine financial system to fund terrorist cells in Europe, Asia, Africa, and the Americas. The driving purpose is to depose Islamic regimes that are friendly with the West and declare jihad upon non-Islamic countries who are a threat.[18]

The Taliban and their supporters presented the Muslim world with new levels of extremism. The growth of the Taliban in Pakistan pushing it toward the extremism of Afghanistan began in 1998. By mid October that year, Pakistan was an Islamist theocracy that was dedicated to the militant spread of Islam. At any given time, over 540,000 Taliban students were taking classes in schools dominated by militant ulema.[19] Pakistani Taliban groups imposed the Shariah punishments of stoning and amputation and banned televisions and videos. They also forced women to adopt the Taliban strict dress code.[20]

During 1999, Jordanian Islamist scholars published a study on the importance of the jihad. The report stressed that the main threat to Islam is the spread of Westernization because it is how the West is expanding its pollution into the Muslim world. The scholars not only included the jihad as a pillar of Islam, but also emphasized that it's currently *needed* as the uppermost part of Islamic law. The hub of Islam must choose to fight for Islam or succumb to the West.[21]

Modern Islamic Civil Wars

There has been an explosion of Islamic conflict worldwide. In 1992, Algeria had an outburst when the Armed Islamic Group (GIA) rebelled against the National Liberation Front, the hegemony of the Islamic secular nationalist party. The GIA massacred entire villages. They targeted journalists, intellectuals, and religious and secular leaders.[22] The terrorists have also harmed "shameless women," trained jurists, and foreign technicians. As of 1998, the civil war had cost up to 60,000 lives.[23]

During the same time, civil war also broke out in Afghanistan. Traditionally, the country had been tolerant to various Muslim sects, as well as other religions and even modernity. What emerged from the ferocious civil war was an end to tolerance and the beginning of strangely divided sects and ethnic groups. In 1995, Ahmad Shah Masud, the Mujahideen leader, massacred the Persian-speaking Hazaras, a Muslim ethnic group. The Hazaras returned the favor to the Taliban in Mazar in 1997, but they got it right back in 1998. Author Ahmed Rashid, in his book *Taliban*, states, "The Taliban's deliberate anti-Shia program has denigrated Islam and the unity of the country as minority groups tried to flee the country en masse. For the first time in Afghanistan's history the unifying factor of Islam has become a lethal weapon in the hands of extremists, a force for division, fragmentation and enormous blood-letting."[24]

In 781, seven thousand Greeks were enslaved after a battle at Ephesus.

Lashkar-i-Tuiba, a well-armed Pakistani Islamic group, took the fight into Indian Kashmir. Another group, the Markaz-al-Daawa wal-Irshad, held a massive rally to advocate violence and terrorism against the Jews and Christians. Their leader, Professor Haviz Mohammad Saeed, stated that jihad was not terrorism but the only solution for world peace against the brutality of Jews and Christians. "The White House is the source of all mischief in the world"[25]

The list of accounts of violence, skirmishes, and Islamic civil wars in the last decade would not be complete without mentioning Indonesia, where thousands of Christians are at risk. In November 2001, Christian Aid reported that over 50,000 Christians were in grave jeopardy in central Sulawesi Island, Indonesia. Islamic Jihad forces, partial to bin Laden's style of revenge, surrounded and brutalized the villagers.[26]

The Weeping Continues

WOMEN

David Landes, historian, economist, and author of *The Wealth and Poverty of Nations*, relates that although some Muslim countries—like Turkey, Egypt, and Iran—have given women the vote, they have not shared any real power:

> The economic implications of gender discrimination are most serious. To deny women, is to deprive a country of labor and talent. . . . In general, the best clue to a nation's growth and development potential is the status and role of women. This is the greatest handicap of Muslim Middle Eastern societies today, the flaw that most bars them from modernity. . . . The women are humiliated from birth. The message: their very existence is a disaster, their body a sin. The boys learn that they can hit their sisters, older and younger, with impunity."[27]

Shariah Law has always leaned toward extreme, unforgiving judgment. For instance, in October 2001, A Shariah court in northern Nigeria sentenced a nursing woman, Safiya Hussani, to death for adultery. Her sentence was commuted until she finished weaning her baby. What happened to the man? The male adulterer, Yakubu Abubakar, was acquitted.[28]

Up to 75% of Muslim women must suffer female circumcision in the most barbaric fashion. More than that are illiterate.[29] Men can marry four women, but women can only marry one man. In divorce, it is often the male who decides the living arrangements of the children.

DECADENCE

Regarding the vast oil wealth of Muslim countries, Author David Landes says,

> The huge oil windfall has been a monumental misfortune. It has intoxicated rulers, henchmen, and purveyors, who have slept on piles of money, wasted it on largely worthless projects, and managed to exceed their figuratively (but not literally) limitless resources. Even Saudi Arabia cannot balance its books. In the process these spoilers have infuriated the Muslim poor, who in turn have sought an outlet for rage and outrage in fundamentalist doctrine.[30]

SLAVERY

Slave trafficking was endorsed in Lebanon right up into the 1970s. In the 1960s in Saudi Arabia, 15,000 people were being imported every year. In the mid 1980s, Africans were still being tricked into visiting Mecca before being abducted. In his book, *Islam's Black Slaves,* Ronald Segal points out that the only reason Saudi Arabia is not currently trafficking in slavery has been the multitude of temporary Asian settlers. These contract laborers practice a form of servitude that closely resembles slavery, making slavery itself superfluous.[31]

Even though world pressure to end slavery exists, Sudan and the Islamic Republic of Mauritania still have hundreds of thousands of slaves. Dr. Hassan al-Turabi and his National Islamic Front (NIF) brought great repression to Sudan in the 1990s. Although he did not reintroduce slavery, it ran unchecked. Information about it is guarded, but some things are known. For instance, in the early nineties, Arab militias used Dinka and Nuba captives as slaves.

Reports show that in May 1994, 150 children were auctioned at Manyeil. In March 1995, over 300 women and children were abducted from a Nuba village and another 248 from a Dinka village and later sold at auction. Herders and farmers normally buy girls for sexual pleasures, and boys for hard work.[32]

In the late 1990s, the Swiss-based Christian Solidarity International (CSI) actually bought freedom for thousands of slaves.[33]

CHAPTER 11

CHRISTIAN JIHAD?

Setting: India, 1825.

Deacon Abdul Masih leaned on the pulpit. Perspiration glistened on his forehead. Although pale and feeble, he continued to impress upon his congregation. "Friends, it has been my joy to serve you here in Agra. As you know, the doctor says my health will not recover unless I find a better climate. I appreciate those of you who came today to say goodbye. For the Muslims, I have a gift. It's a tract about a conversation between Jesus and Nicodemus. Consider it closely. Who else in all of Islamic tradition is like Jesus? Thanks to the translation by Henry Martin, you can read the Gospels for yourself and learn Jesus is the Son of God."

The preacher steadied himself and took a sip of water.

"Consider how many lives have been changed by the obedience of one missionary. Some thought Henry Martin came from England with Christian zeal that ended without fruit. When he asked me to bind his New Testament translation, he was discouraged. Not one Muslim had yet converted. Before he died, I never told him that I had listened to him teach the beggars near the Taj

Mahal. Perhaps, he thought no one had heard. But I did. I read the New Testament and accepted Jesus into my life. Prior to that, as Sheikh Salith, I enjoyed importance in King Oudh's court. None of it compared to the important freedom I found in Christ.

"Many have helped me along the way. Reverend Brown and Reverend Corrie—I thank God for them. Yet, today, it is fitting to dedicate all of this to the memory of Henry Martin. I am his legacy, as are you, as are the various translations that will touch thousands, and the school, hymns, tracts, and even your jobs here. His Urdu translation of the New Testament will accomplish much more in the generations to come. We Muslims can be a stubborn bunch. But the passion, determination, and sacrifices of one man changed that.

"Now, who will come to Christ through your efforts? Brothers and sisters, your lives are important. Count the cost. Live so that your light shines the truth into the hearts of Muslims and others."

Abdul stopped. His gaze shifted to a portrait of Christ hanging on the cross. "What about the Christian efforts over the generations to reach the Muslims? I am sure that the Lord has always had his anonymous saints reaching out to Muslims, with great result. Yet, I also think of those who, like Henry Martin, obeyed God but never saw the fruit. Consider the great missionary efforts of Raymund Lull, who, in the fourteenth century, was eventually martyred in Tunis by Muslims. There had been no converts at the time. Even Francis of Assisi went to the Sultan of Egypt during the thirteenth century and preached the gospel. How bold, but no one converted! These men *seemed* to have little impact, but God knows the truth. Their lives stood for Christ, the seed were planted, and people were eventually influenced.

"Francis of Assisi once said, 'Preach the gospel always; if necessary, use words.' That is what I want to leave with you. Live your lives so that people can see Christ's gospel through your actions. Pray for them. Then, when the right time appears, tell them about Jesus."

✡ ✞ ☪

Abbas Abhari discovered the compassion of the Lord Jesus Christ in an interesting way. As a proud Muslim cleric in the town of Damghan, he heard that a Christian missionary, Ivan Wilson, was telling people about Jesus. Abbas decided to illustrate the superiority of Islam by humiliating the missionary in debate. Mr. Wilson received Abbas kindly, and the debate reached a stalemate when Abbas clung to the usual Muslim responses: "No, Jesus was not God's Son. . . . He did not die on the cross. . . . He foretold the coming of Muhammad. . . . The Christian Scriptures have been corrupted. . . . Christians worship three gods."

Years later in an interview, Abbas explained what finally changed him:

> Mr. Wilson came here, he talked with me and argued with me, but I felt I had overcome him, and I was feeling very proud of myself. Then that man of God felt so sorry for me in my unbelief and pride that he began to weep. His tears did for me what his arguments did not do. They melted my heart, and I believed and became a Christian. Later, I was baptized.[1]

True Christians need to express brokenness and humility when dealing with those of unbelief. One man said, "Real spirituality will express itself in tears when souls are erring into destruction."[2] Likewise, Jesus wept over the unbelief of those in Jerusalem. His entire ministry was an intercession for them. The Apostle Paul served the Lord with humility and tears (Acts 20:19) and wept for the enemies of the cross (Philippians 3:18).

When the World Trade Center collapsed and thousands died on September 11, 2001, cries went up all over the world on behalf of the victims and their families. Many Christians found themselves also praying and weeping that the perpetrators would come to know the truth about Jesus. That is the weapon of spiritual warfare. Christians are instructed "not to wrestle against flesh and blood" but to fight the demonic principalities (Ephesians 6:10–12). The following deal with different aspects of Christian warfare:

> For though we walk in the flesh, we do not war according to the flesh. For the weapons of our warfare are not carnal but mighty in God for pulling down strongholds, casting down arguments and every high thing that exalts itself against the knowledge of God, bringing every thought into captivity to the obedience of Christ, and being ready to punish all disobedience when your obedience is fulfilled. (2 Corinthians 10:3–6)

> He who kills with the sword must be killed with the sword. Here is the patience and the faith of the saints. (Revelation 13:10)

The true weapons of Christians are spiritual, not physical—a much different manner than Islam spreads its message. Christian spiritual weapons are *mighty* in God. The word *mighty* is from the Greek *dunatos*, meaning "powerful" or "capable." This has the same root as the word *dynamite*. The spiritual weapons of God are of greater potency in God's eyes than swords, guns, suicide bombers, or any demonic stronghold. Even though those principalities have bound Islamic rationale in deceit, they cannot ultimately overcome the truth of Jesus Christ. He is the "head of all principality and power" (Colossians 2:10).

Perhaps the Bible has a better handle on the true spiritual jihad than even the Koran. A Christian jihad would be "an inner struggle for submission to God combined with an outward resistance that overcomes the devil and his dominion." This is a major part of the Christian calling.

In the late 1980s, David Shibley told of the need for global evangelism by Christians. He made an insightful point about the growing openness among Muslims to the gospel:

> Millions of Muslims are embarrassed by Islam's more belligerent exponents. This has produced widespread discontent as more and more Muslims search for a true knowledge of God and His ways. While it cannot be said that Muslims are yet turning to Christ in massive numbers, it is true that more seeking Muslims are coming to Christ than ever before. . . . It seems clear that most religions are becoming more militant. Christianity as well is becoming more militant but with an important difference. Our aggression is motivated by love, not hate. And our arsenal is not material, but spiritual.[3]

The Church may have a golden opportunity to harvest the ripe souls as confused Muslims genuinely critique their own faith.

Three major weapons that Christians have are prayer, love, and witnessing. Through these, countless people have come to know Jesus Christ as Savior and Lord. Nations and destinies have been changed. These spiritual missiles can bring a new kind of jihad, one that lays bare the faulty ideologies and demonic principalities of Islam.

Jihad of Prayer

The great prayer warrior E. M. Bounds said:

> Prayer is of transcendent importance. Prayer is the mightiest agent to advance God's work. Praying hearts and hands only can do God's work. Prayer succeeds when all else fails. Prayer has won great victories, and rescued, with notable triumph, God's saints when every other hope was gone. Men who know how to pray are the greatest boon God can give to earth—they are the richest gift earth can offer heaven. Men who know how to use this weapon of prayer are God's best soldiers, His mightiest leaders.[4]

In October of 1993, Christians around the world were challenged to pray for the 10 / 40 window and one hundred Gateway cities. The 10 / 40 window is a geographical latitude region encompassing 10 degrees to 40 degrees north of the equator and from western Africa all the way across Asia. Within that region are nearly 3 billion of the world's least evangelized people. The movement became the greatest prayer effort in the history of the world up to that time.[5] As a yearly event, it grew, and by 1995 more than 36 million Christians in 102 nations prayed fervently for God to mightily make Himself known to the spiritually impoverished people in that region of the world.[6]

For years now the Church has been praying for the people in that region of the world. Prayer has impact as it rises up like incense to the throne of God. He is able to heal, secure miracles, encourage from a distance, and thwart demonic plans. Prayer from a humble heart can prevail. For example, in answer to Hezekiah's prayer, an angel slew one hundred and eighty-five thousand of Sennacherib's army in one night (2 Kings 19:35). Is it possible that prayer is dislodging or sorely pricking demonic principalities? Author and speaker George Otis, Jr., proposed the idea that at the epicenter of the unreached world stands two powerful demonic forces of great biblical significance, the prince of Persia (Iran) and the spirit of Babylon (Iraq).[7] Both continue to resist the prayers of the saints.

Ed Silvoso makes an interesting claim about Satan. In his book, *That None Should Perish*, he writes, "Once Satan's camp is infiltrated, he will stage a diversionary counterattack by orchestrating weird demonic manifestations."[8] Although Silvoso did not write this in reference to Islam and terrorism, the principle of it is valid. Could rising terrorist activity be the result of angry principalities that are trying to divert prayer away?

Prayer changes people. Prayer changes nations.

In *Stories from the Front Lines,* author Jane Rumph relates an interesting example of prayer. Simba Mohammadovich, a twenty-three-year-old male, was raised a Sunni Muslim but turned to Sufi Islam (animism) as he grew older due to visions he was having. In 1992, he encountered a Christian named Martha and asked her for a Turkish New Testament. She did not have one but invited him to visit a Messianic Muslim Christian fellowship, so that he could learn more about her faith. He refused on several occasions but finally attended. As a Muslim, Simba thought he knew all about prayer. Five times a day, he normally prayed for himself, his family, and perhaps a close friend. These Christians were different. They were praying for many things and people, including him. Their sincere love oozed into his heart and he could not get the meeting out of his mind. Eventually, he accepted Jesus as his Messiah.[9]

But what is the impact of prayer from afar? Supernatural encounters are happening all over the world. A report by the Institute for Muslim Studies says, "The frequency of reported dreams and visions of Christ among Muslims has dramatically risen in the last 15 years."[10] In China, people are being raised from the dead. In Africa, missionaries have seen supernatural signs and wonders among natives with traditional religions. In Algeria, the Berber Kabyle people are coming to Christ through dreams, visions, and God's Word. A theological seminary reported a study showing that of 100 converts from Islam to Christianity, half acknowledged dreams of a Christian nature either before or soon after conversion.

A Christian in Nigeria was tortured for his faith. While lying on his deathbed, two of the mullahs responsible overheard the man praying and asking forgiveness for his torturers. The following night, both mullahs had visions. Jesus showed one mullah three of his greatest and most secret sins. Both mullahs repented, converted to Christianity, and lead their 80 followers to a church.

A decade ago, at an evangelistic crusade in Pakistan, 2,000 people gave their lives to the Lord, and many miracles were reported: A woman stood up and walked from her wheelchair; a mute person began to speak; a person suffering from mental illness recovered; the grandson of a veterinarian was instantly healed. In Qatar a man whose right foot was crooked was healed.[11] A Muslim blind man in an Albanian hospital requested prayer and was totally healed and then saved. Ziad, a Muslim from Syria, was in Germany for training when his daughter fell ill and was given no hope by doctors. In desperation, he prayed to Jesus for help. His daughter was miraculously healed. Soon Zaid, his wife, and his child accepted Jesus as Lord and Savior.[12]

There are accounts of epileptics getting healed, demons being cast out, and people having personal encounters with Jesus. Many of these events—if not all—can be directly or indirectly tied to someone somewhere praying.[13] A Muslim man named Parviz came to the United States from Tehran with his family. Shaken by Khomeini's ruthlessness, he asked himself, "What does it mean when religion turns people into such monsters?" One night in the midst of culture shock, financial hardship, stress, and a back injury, he slept restlessly. He had a dream of a man in a white robe leading him to a fountain of water and asking him to drink. Shortly after, he awoke and saw a picture of Jesus. It was the man in the dream. Today, he serves that Man.

In 1992, a Muslim on his hajj to the Kabah in Mecca claimed his bus driver told him all about the Bible and Jesus. Later, he discovered that this was not the normal bus driver. He was disturbed by what the man said, and he had difficulty enjoying the hajj or admiring the prophet Muhammad. Later, back in Sumatra, the man visited a Christian and saw a picture of someone's rendition of Jesus. It was the same man he saw driving the bus.[14]

These stories can challenge our Western rationale and ministry approach. Prayer is the key to powerful changes. Churches in America need to continue to pray for the protection and salvation of our nation, our leaders, and the unreached peoples of the world.

Bob Sjogren, the president for Frontier Associations, said in a 1994 interview, "More Muslims have come to know the Lord in the past 25 years than in the entire history of missions to Islam."[15] Today, leaders in the prayer movement are shifting the focus from the 10/40 Window to the 40/70 Window, in order to pray on behalf of the European countries. While Europe is spiritually dark and certainly needs prayer, we should continue to press in on behalf of the 10/40 Window to cover the greatest number of Muslims.

The prayer warrior S. D. Gordon simplified the concept of prayer this way:

> In its simplest meaning prayer has to do with conflict. Rightly understood it is the deciding factor in a spirit conflict. The scene of the conflict is the earth. The purpose of the conflict is to decide the control of the earth, and its inhabitants. The conflict runs back into the misty ages of the creation time. . . . Prayer is man giving God a footing on the contested territory of this earth. The man in full touch of purpose with God praying, insistently praying—that man is God's footing on the enemy's soil. The man wholly given over to God gives Him a new sub-headquarters on the battlefield from which to work out. And the Holy Spirit within that man, on the new spot, will insist on the enemy's retreat in Jesus the Victor's name. That is prayer. Shall we not, every one of us, increase God's footing down upon His prodigal earth![16]

As Christians, we are to pray for all men everywhere (1 Timothy 2:1–2). That includes our neighbors, communities, leaders, nation, and the countries of the world. John Chrysostom (AD 350–407) wrote why, and it is still valid for the Church today:

> The potency of prayer hath subdued the strength of fire; it hath bridled the rage of lions, hushed anarchy to rest, extinguished wars, appeased the elements, expelled demons, burst the chains of death, expanded the gates of heaven, assuaged diseases, repelled frauds, rescued cities from destruction, stayed the sun in its course, and arrested the progress of the thunderbolt.[17]

Jihad of Love

The Bible teaches us:

- "God is Love" (1 John 4:16)
- "We love Him because He first loved us" (1 John 4:19)

- To speak "the truth in love" (Ephesians 4: 15)
- "For God so loved the world that He sent His only begotten Son" (John 3:16)

God is the essence of love. The reason we are able to even know and express genuine love is because He loves us. Many do not know of His love or accept the gift of His Son. We are to speak the truth to them in a spirit of charity.

Sometimes people misjudge or don't understand the love of Christians. Yet, that love has birthed many generations of missions, charity hospitals, food ministries, and prayer teams for Muslims and others. Love is a weapon in God's arsenal that disarms the toughest assailant and melts the hardest heart.

Shahrokh Afshar became a pastor at a Christian church for Iranians in Los Angeles. However, when he first came to the States, he argued his position with Christians. It was the love he saw in their lives that melted him. A Christian friend invited him to Thanksgiving dinner, and the simple prayer of a father saying grace touched him.[18] From simple social gatherings and warm acceptance, this brother gave his life to Christ.

There are a host of ministries to Muslims from Christians, such as:

- Frontier Associations
- the Zwemler Institute of Muslim Studies
- Arab World Ministries
- 30 Days Muslim Prayer Focus and Missionary Action / Flame
- Arabic Bible Outreach Ministry

There are also organizations like World Relief, World Vision, and others that include strong Christian outreach with food, clothing, education, and other practical needs. Churches also send missionaries. Denominations have entire branches of ministry dedicated to Muslim people groups. That is love.

Author Steve Sjogren wrote about love and deeds:

> Deeds of kindness get people's attention and often cause them to ask questions. Instead of having a forced presentation of the gospel to people who really aren't interested in what you have to say, we find people are curious and ask us to explain the message, which is vital to bringing someone to Christ without taking a sales approach. When we do speak we must be sensitive to the level of receptivity of each person and explain the words of God's love in whatever way the hearer can understand. These words are the cognitive or conscious element of our evangelism. If we don't follow our actions with words, they will only know that we are nice people, not that God loves them.[19]

Jihad of Witnessing

Despite an overt contempt for the West, there seems to be a growing openness to the gospel in Muslim countries. One believer who returned from Syria and Lebanon tells of mighty miracles. "When giving out our *Who is Jesus!* tracts, the people, even those involved with the Hezbollah terrorists, take them tenderly in their hands and kiss them, exclaiming after they read them, 'This is the Good News that we have been waiting for!' They refuse to let the tracts out of their hands."[20]

In Iraq, a young man named Monthir was searching for Jesus in the Koran and read Sura 10:94 "And if thou art in doubt as to what we have sent down to thee, inquire at those who have read the Scriptures before thee." So he got a Bible and discovered John 14:6, "I am the way, the truth, and life. No one comes to the Father except through Me." Monthir gave his life to Jesus.[21]

In Egypt, a Christian was summoned to pray for a sick woman at the house of a devoted and influential Muslim fundamentalist leader. The Christian was afraid but went anyway. After she prayed with the ailing woman, the fundamentalist followed the Christian out to her car and got in. At first, she was fearful. Then she was amazed to hear of the heavenly vision he had seen a few nights earlier. The Lord Jesus had told the man that His blood was shed for him. He told his Islamic fundamentalist group of 150 about what happened, and they all decided to follow Al-Masih Isa.[22]

Hatred of the Jews did not begin with the establishment of modern day Israel, it is in the soul of Islam.

Christians have been sending missionaries to Muslim countries for centuries. During the colonial period, Western countries sometimes had Muslim conversion in mind when they colonized various countries. This was resented by the umma and ulema, as were any conversions of Muslims to Christianity. Education was considered to be the key in some places. Western society thought that if Muslims became educated, they would see the truth of Christianity. The American University in Beirut started as a Christian missionary foundation. Hospitals, medical clinics, and other charities were used as a social gospel of love to open hearts to the evangelical gospel.[23]

However, it can be hard to witness to people who face the threat of being shunned or being killed for converting to Christianity. Similarly, many Christians have given their lives to the cause of seeing Muslims come to Christ. Regarding hardcore communities like those in Saudi Arabia, especially in Mecca, one study concluded that the best way to reach them is to mobilize converted Muslim nationals, train them, disciple them, and then send them back into the country to plant underground churches.[24]

There is also the simple yet powerful witness of the Bible. Sometimes the Word—all by itself—leads people to the truth. Author William Miller tells of one such case:

> One day a shoemaker in Meshed brought home for his lunch some cheese which the grocer had wrapped in a page of the New Testament, which he was using for wrapping paper. After eating lunch Qasim picked up the piece of paper and read the story of the man who hired laborers for his vineyard, and at the end of day paid all the laborers the same wage, whether they had worked twelve hours or one. Qasim liked the story, and next day went again to the grocery store and bought cheese, asking that it be wrapped in another page of that book. Finally, on the third day he bought what remained of the New Testament and showed it to his brother. The two of them then went to the missionary, who gave them a complete copy, and also gave them regular instruction in the Word of God. Both men were later baptized and were among the first believers in Meshed.[25]

There is no true salvation in Islam. A girl who stood in front of a Muslim judge in a Shariah court was asked, "Why did you leave Islam?"

"Because there is no salvation in Islam."

The judge turned to his advisors, experts in Islamic law, and asked them, "Is this true?" After consulting together they answered that it was. The judge turned to the girl and said, "There is no case. You are free to go."[26]

While it would be inaccurate to say that all Muslims think Islam lacks salvation, the Muslim idea of salvation does not compare to the salvation offered by Christianity. Islam salvation is based on works. The salvation of Christians is based solely on the work of Christ at Calvary.

Christians should never underestimate the spiritual weapons of prayer, love, and witnessing. We were given the sword of His Word, so that Muslims all over the world can hear the good news of salvation in Jesus Christ.

CHAPTER 12

FORTRESS OF PEACE

Setting: A medical laboratory in modern-day Cairo.

The lab was hot. Poor ventilation combined with the weight of a full-body veil caused Hanan to perspire heavily. Trying to peer into the microscope, her glasses continued to steam. She wiped them and quickly tried to get a look at the bacteria. If only she knew whether or not the new assistant, Mohamed, was going to come back, she could remove the veil and get her work done. Unsure, she decided against it. Her extensive background in microbiology helped to identify the specimen quickly as her mind wandered in secret debates with her husband, Zahi.

The marriage contract she had signed years ago granted him permission to marry others, but she never thought he would—especially a non-Muslim. *Why a Jew?* Sure, Sarah was pretty, especially compared to Hanan's aging features. *It just isn't fair. Why can't I marry a non-Muslim man? There will be no peace in the house at all.*

Hanan became so absorbed in thought she ignored her task momentarily and opened a drawer. Inside was a New Testament that Dr. Ahmed had boldly given her in the staff cafeteria. She had almost refused but did not want to cause any awkwardness with this well respected man. He seemed nice—for a Christian.

Dr. Ahmed had pointed out that the tensions around Israel had been predicted in the Bible and might even mean that Jesus is returning soon. *Maybe I should convert to Christianity. That would teach Zahi. He would be a Muslim professor with a Christian and a Jew for his wives!* She laughed out loud and it startled her. She knew it would mean certain persecution.

She knew why Zahi was going to marry this girl. *Her selfish brother just wants to marry her off so he doesn't have to provide for her. And why doesn't she have to wear a veil? Zahi never would have noticed her in the store if she had to wear one. . . . If only I could have given him children."*

She snapped back to work. It was important. She was a fine scientist, one who was helping to discover the cures for many sick people.

A few minutes later, Hanan was in the process of labeling various slides when her aide walked into the room with some trays. "So are you and Zahi going to the dinner for the descendents of the Mamlûk chiefs tonight?"

"Yes. Obligations, you know. We are descendents of two chiefs that were actually friends—that is, before being butchered."

Mohamed tried to make a joke, "Yeah, wasn't that also a dinner party?"

Hanan stuck to the facts. "Yes, all 480 were slain by Muhammad Ali in 1811. He certainly changed the destiny of Egypt for all of us."

"That's some kind of modernization program," Mohamed replied. He pondered his own words for a moment. "I wonder if we've changed much, with all the assassinations and suicide terrorists." It didn't matter as much as what he remembered. "Did you hear who is singing there tonight? Shaaban Abdel Rahim! He'll sing his new song, 'I love Amr Moussa, and I hate Israel.' Talk about an explosive beat!"

Hanan was a little shocked. No, she did not know that singer and she had not heard his new song. But the title suggested the evening could be fun after all. The part about loving Amr Moussa, the charismatic leader of the Arab League, was laughable. But the other part was . . . perfect.

As soon as Mohamed left the room, Hanan dialed the phone. "Zahi? Yes, I have been thinking. We can invite guests to the party tonight, right? Well, perhaps I have been a bit hard on Sarah. We should invite her as an act of friendship. . . . Oh, it would be *so* good. Okay, give her a call and tell her to dress up. We need to get there in plenty of time to get three good seats for the entertainment. . . . Yes, of course I'm going to enjoy it. I can't wait, dear."

Abdulrahman lived in Iraq with his parents and was a descendent of Caliph Ali, the cousin of Muhammad. One night he dreamed a man with a beard said to him, "Son, why do you attack my sheep?"

Abdulrahman replied, "Who are you sir?"

"Jesus Christ."

The young man thought for a moment. Then he said, "I'm not attacking your sheep, Sir. I'm trying to bring Your lost sheep back to the straight path."

Jesus said, "You are the one who is lost; I'm the straight path."

After waking up, Abdulrahman was impressed with the dream, but he did not immediately become a Christian. He did, however, disregard Islam.

Sometime in 1990, after a tragic automobile accident that killed Abdulrahman's father, Isa said to him, "Run away from your country now!" He obeyed. After arriving at his grandfather's home in another country, he contacted his mother, who told him never to come home. He learned that his father, a high-ranking officer, had been assassinated and that the police had just come to arrest Abdulrahman because they thought he had knowledge of secret military documents hidden by his father. The shock of this information combined with the merciful revelations by Isa convinced Abdulrahman the Prince of Peace was the true spiritual direction for his life.[1]

Not all Muslims who convert to Christianity are prompted by the Lord to escape silently. Many are shunned by their family and face cruel treatment from Islamic extremists. Authors Paul and Frances Hiebert, in their book *Case Studies in Missions*, reveal the tremendous pressures Muslims face when converting. One story tells of Malika, who gave her life to Al-Masih Isa, "the Messiah Jesus," in Cairo and was baptized. Afterward, she willingly gave her testimony at churches and home meetings. Then, the secret police started harassing her. A zealous lieutenant named Hassan, known for his cruelty, summoned her for interrogation. Malika was concerned not only for herself, but also for her family and those she had led to the Lord.[2] Persecution underlines the cost of conversion to Christianity. This type of pressure can hush new Christians who don't want to hurt their families or traditions. Instead, they pray for their loved ones and the right time to tell them.

Hijacking the Mind

David Minor, a well-respected pastor, once defined *stronghold* as a system of thinking that, if held long enough, becomes easy for demonic powers to reinforce.[3] Consider five points that help define a stronghold.[4]

1. STRONGHOLDS ARE IN THE MIND. Muslims do not challenge their faith in Islam. They are taught to believe and obey. This system prohibits an honest evaluation of those beliefs.

2. THEY CAN BE BASED ON GOOD THOUGHTS. Anyone can justify his or her own thoughts—even pious ones. It doesn't mean those thoughts are true.
3. THEY OFTEN DEVELOP IN THE SHADOW OF OUR STRENGTH. Muslims encourage many good deeds and a pious lifestyle that helps to drown the doubts in their minds.
4. THEY ARE OFTEN ACTIVATED BY TRAUMA. Trauma, in this case, is an increase in Islamic terrorism. Muslims are lured into irrational thinking that deludes them of any relationship to Islamic extremism.
5. THEY CAUSE SPIRITUAL AND EMOTIONAL INSTABILITY. For Muslims, genuine curiosity is stifled quickly in a quagmire of traditions. The truth is deflected away, as if it was a tempting dart from Shaitan. The battle of the heart can be twisted and acted out through the guise of jihad. Confused Muslims think they have overcome when, in fact, they have been overcome by a great deception.

Choices

The violence of Islamic terrorists is creating an instability and subtle polarization within the minds of peaceful Muslims, whom have already been struggling to be understood by their non-Muslim neighbors. These kinds of circumstances often reveal the true character and heart of a people—and force hard decisions to be made.

Muslims reacted to the September attack and the war with Afghanistan in predictable fashion: hurt, embarrassment, justification, anger, and political splintering. For instance, in the U.S., Sheik Muhammad Gemeaha, a scholar with Cairo's prominent al-Azhar University and the leader of the Islamic Cultural Center in New York City, made the outlandish claim that Jews were the ones who carried out the attack on the WTC and were poisoning Muslim children in U.S. hospitals. He resigned his position and fled to Cairo.

The U.S. board of the Islamic Cultural Center reacted to his bogus views and cut off its longstanding relationship with al-Azhar University and its fifty-year oversight of the U.S. center.[5]

The people of Kuwait also chose a new direction. They had been supportive of the United States for protecting them against the Iraqi invasion. Yet, after America's attack on the Taliban, many condemned the war against the Taliban and Osama bin Laden. A large percentage of the population esteems him as a freedom fighter. Kuwaitis have accused the United States of having anti-Arab media and partiality to Jews.[6] On the other hand, countries like Pakistan, once struggling with U.S. policy, helped overthrow the Taliban—and exposed the extreme divisions within their own country. As part of the backlash, sixteen Christians were assassinated at St. Dominic's church in Bahawalpur in October 2001.[7]

Choices abound for Christians, as well, and those decisions will expose what is in the heart. For many Christians, issues such as the reclamation of Israel by the Jews in 1948, the Palestinian question, nuclear weapons, biological warfare, and growing religious differences bring the possibility of Armageddon to the forefront. No one really knows when Armageddon will take place, but violence will increase and it will test the patience of the saints. Scripture alludes to the premise that Armageddon will be a literal battle fought in the Middle East, somewhere in the vicinity of Jerusalem. The entire world will take part. However, the Bible emphasizes the *spiritual* conflict between the forces of Shaitan and the heavenly forces of Isa (Jesus).

Yet, how should we respond? There is a growing openness today, even in Islamic countries. Christians need to fill that gap with the love of Jesus. In Pakistan, Andreas Huebner, evangelist and founder of a German-based ministry called Jesus to the World Mission, is seeing thousands come to the Lord and get healed. Upon entering Pakistan, Huebner asked the Pakistan Gospel Assemblies for assistance. This organization includes upward of 2,000 charismatic house churches in Pakistan. In September 2000, at one of his meetings, he asked how many had received physical healing. Some 5,000 new converts raised their hands.[8] Isa cares greatly for the Muslim people—and more need to hear about it!

The Maze

Finding the right path to truth should be everyone's goal. Unfortunately, many religions and philosophies make it difficult by creating mazes for people to follow. Corridors lead into different paths, sometimes crisscrossing, sometimes separating into more complex ideologies. To simplify the maze, some people claim all ways lead to truth—which is pure speculation. There is no verifiable evidence to support that view.

Christianity offers something more: a straight path to Jesus Christ, who said, "I am the way, the truth, and the life. No one comes to the Father except through Me" (John 14:6).

The heaven of Islam is full of female virgins ready to fulfill the sexual needs of faithful Muslim men.

Muslims can get confused trying to understand the many Christian denominations. Phil Parshall makes an insightful comment in his book *The Cross and the Crescent*. While visiting the town of Midsayap, in Mindanao, Philippines, he noted that on the main street there was one Muslim mosque compared to following churches:

- Four Square Gospel
- Church of Jesus Christ of Latter-day saints
- Roman Catholic
- United Church of the Philippines

- Southern Baptists
- Church of the Deliverance
- Christian and Missionary Alliance.[9]

Mature Christians can understand the differences in that list as Catholic, mainstream denominations, one independent, and a cult. Yet, what is a Muslim to think? If all Christian cults, sects, denominations, independents, and other meeting places simply titled themselves as a *church*, Muslims would better understand the comparison to *mosque*.

But once converted, Muslims may still wonder how to practice Christianity. There is a lot of variety. From childhood, Muslims are taught strict rituals on exactly how and when to pray, which direction to face, when to attend the mosque, how much to give, what to think, what to wear, and what to say. The ritual practices of Christianity are not nearly so set. People pray when, what, where, and how they want. Church service schedules vary. Also, people worship the Lord in different styles, according to the church they attend. The bottom line? Christians have freedom to live for and relate to the person of Jesus Christ, Al-Masih Isa. The emphasis is not on *how* it is done, but *who* is receiving the worship. A personal, living relationship with the Lord Jesus Christ is what connects Christians, regardless of church affiliation.

The Koran acknowledges that Isa was the Messiah, a prophet, miracle worker, and miraculously born of the Virgin Mary. It also accepts the divine inspiration of the Torah, the Psalms, and the Gospels of Isa (Sura 2:79). Yet, it denies that Isa is the Son of God and that God is the Heavenly Father. If Isa was God in the flesh, and Muslims deny Him, then to whom are Muslims actually praying?

The True Way: Al-Masih Isa

Muslims argue that Shariah Law puts them on the right way. Jews say the Torah puts them on the right way. Buddhists teach that they are on the middle way (not worldly, not ascetic); Baha'i and Hindus think that all religions have the right way.

Jesus said that He is the only way.

Jews and Muslims have a religion based on works: They try to live holy lives based on their scriptural laws. Christianity is based on faith: Believers try to live through Christ's righteousness, accepting forgiveness for their sin and rejoicing in the free gift of salvation that comes through the substitution of Jesus Christ on the cross.

The Bible says that sin separates us from God (Isaiah 59:2) and that all men have sinned (Romans 3:23). God is sovereign and may extend His grace on judgment day to those who tried to live a good life of works by the laws of Judaism and Islam before the Lord (Romans 2:12–16), but why wait? Jesus came to be the hope of everyone. He received the penalty of sin for *all* people who will receive Him. It's as simple as that.

Fortress of Peace

The historic worldview of Islam separated the world into two realms: *Dar-al-Islam* (House of Islam, or House of Peace) and *Dar-al-Harb* (House of War).[10] Islam condones war against everything outside of Islam. This has dominated Islam since its inception. Today, it threatens the safety of modern civilization and, after September 11th, has left many people fearful.

Those who have come to know Jesus as Savior and Lord have found something much better than fear. The Apostle Paul wrote about it to his disciple Timothy, "For God has not given us a sprit of fear, but of power and of love and of a sound mind" (2 Timothy 1:7). Christians have a way to overcome fear after all, "God is not the author of confusion but of peace" (1 Corinthians 14:33). Peace is important to God and was expressly emphasized by Isa. On the night of the Last Supper, while warning the disciples that He would soon be betrayed, he said,

> Peace I leave with you. My peace I give to you; not as the world gives do I give to you. Let not your heart be troubled, neither let it be afraid. . . . These things I have spoken to you, that in Me you may have peace. In the world you will have tribulation, but be of good cheer. I have overcome the world. (John 14:29; 16:33)

In Isaiah 9:6 Jesus is called the "Prince of Peace." He provides a mighty fortress against the principalities and powers of demonic forces. He offers true peace, even at times of intense stress.

After His resurrection, Jesus spoke to His disciples, "Peace be with you" (John 20:19). It is interesting to note that He spoke these words with the full knowledge that his disciples had previously abandoned Him in His hour of need, when Jesus was facing crucifixion. The Lord's openness to forgive and receive them should not have surprised the disciples. He had often done so.

Right now, the peace of Jesus is available for all who are willing to accept Him as Lord. During the Last Supper, Jesus prayed not only for those disciples who were present, but also for those who would believe in Him in the future.

> I do not pray for these alone, but also for those who will believe in Me through their word; that they all may be one, as You, Father, are in Me, and I in You; that they also may be one in Us, that the world may believe that You sent Me. And the glory which You gave Me I have given them, that they may be one just as We are one: I in them, and You in Me; that they may be made perfect in one, and that the world may know that You have sent Me, and have loved them as You have loved Me. Father, I desire that they also whom You gave Me may be with Me where I am, that they may behold My glory which You have given Me; for You loved Me before the foundation of the world! O righteous Father! The world has not known You, but I have known You; and these have known that You sent Me. And I have declared to them Your name, and will declare it, that the love with which You loved Me may be in them, and I in them. (John 17:20–28)

When you ask Isa into your heart, He speaks peace into your life. He gives hope that calms the fears. He is the Master of the fortress of peace, and has opened the door for anyone to be close to Him. His words transform lives, heal hearts, and can change destiny.

> Let him who thirsts come. Whoever desires, let him take the water of life freely. (Revelation 22:17)

A Call to Action for Christians

Today, God is reaching out to Muslims through dreams, visions, and miracles to show them the truth about Jesus (Al-Masih Isa). As Christians, we have a great opportunity to pray and see the Lord move. If you come into contact with Muslims, pray for them. Christians in the U.S. have the unique opportunity of sharing with the many Muslims who attend our universities. These individuals can make an immediate impact in their home Islamic countries. Christians need to send out missionaries continuously to Muslim countries to start Bible studies and cell churches. If you are a church leader, ask the Lord, "What can our church do to reach Muslims?" Make the commitment and stick to it.

ENDNOTES

Chapter 1

1 Some disparity exists in the event timeline between different news sources. For this volume, www.cnn.com has been chosen.

2 Mindy Belz, *World Magazine*, “We are the world”, September 22, 2001, 32.

3 CNN Special Report: The Relativities and the Rhetoric, aired October 14, 2001 (8:00 PST).

4 From Internet statistics: www. adherents.com/rel_USA.html#religions

5 Josh Tyrangiel, *Time Magazine*, “Did You Hear About”, October 8, 2001, 77.

Chapter 2

1 From the Anti-Defamation League Internet Site, Profile of Osama bin Laden, adl.org/terrorism_America/bin_l.asp

2 www.cnn.com—a bin Laden time line.

3 Anti-Defamation League Internet Site, Profile of Osama bin Laden.

4 Mindy Belz, *World Magazine*, 34.

5 David E. Kaplan and Kevin Whitelaw, *U.S. News & World Report*, “The CEO of Terror Inc.”, October 1, 2001, 19.

6 Walter M. Weiss, *Islam: an Illustrated Historical Overview* (Hauppauge, NY: Published by Barron's Educational Series, Inc., 2000), 162.

7 Karen Armstrong, *Islam: A short History* (New York, NY: Random House, 2000), 164.

8 John L. Esposito, Islamic Threat: Myth or Reality? Third Edition (New York, NY: Oxford University Press, 1999), 5–6.

9 CNN Special Report: The Relativities and the Rhetoric.

10 Esposito, 221.

11 CNN Special Report: The Relativities and the Rhetoric.
12 Kaplan and Whitelaw, *U.S. News & World Report*, 22.
13 CNN Special Report: The Relativities and the Rhetoric.
14 Osama bin Laden, *World Islamic Front Statement*, from Cornell University Internet library files, February 23, 1998.
15 Osama bin Laden, ibid.

Chapter 3

1 Ahmed Rashid, *Taliban: Militant Islam, Oil, & Fundamentalism in Central Asia* (New Haven: Yale University Press, 2001), 13, 18.
2 Yossef Bodansky, *Bin Laden: The Man Who Declared War on America* (Roseville, CA: Prima Publishing, 2001), 28–29.
3 Weiss, 161.
4 Bodansky, 30.
5 Rashid, 133.
6 Ed Decker quoting from New York Times magazine (March 10, 1991) in *Understanding Islam: The Mystery Religion* (A paper published by Ed Decker, November, 2001), 8.
7 Quote from Ron Carlson, President of Christian Ministries International, renowned expert on world religions; in my personal e-mail file.
8 Richard Booker, *Blow the Trumpet in Zion* (Shippensburg, PA: Destiny Image Publishers, 1992)
9 www.us-israel.org—relationship between the United States and Israel.
10 www.us-israel.org—quoting the *Los Angeles Times*, September 20, 2001.
11 Weiss, 82.
12 *Hadith*, vol. 1, nos. 211, 345.
13 Tim Dowley, editor, *Eerdman's Handbook to the History of Christianity* (Grand Rapids, MI: Wm. B. Eerdman's Publishing Co., 1977), 54.
14 Clarence H. Wagner, Jr., *Christianity Today*, "Between a Rock and a Holy Site", February 5, 2001, 62–63.
15 Esposito, 118.
16 Weiss, 163-164.
17 www.us-israel.org—timeline
18 Armstrong, 176.
19 Rashid, 211–212.

Chapter 4

1 *The Koran*, translated by J. M. Rodwell (Rutland, VT: Charles E. Tuttle Co. Inc., 1994), 37.
2 James Strong, *The New Strong's Exhaustive Concordance of the Bible*, (Nashville, TN: Thomas Nelson Publishers, 1995).

3 Adam Clarke, *Adam Clarke's Commentary on the Holy Bible* (Grand Rapids, MI: Baker Book House, 1987).

4 *Josephus: Complete Works*, translated by W. Whiston (Grand Rapids, MI: Kregel Publications, 1980), 36.

5 Armstrong, 17.

6 Weiss, 12.

7 Anne Cooper, *Ishmael My Brother: A Christian Introduction to Islam* (Crowborough, East Sussex, Great Britain: MARC, an imprint of Monarch Publications, 1997), 102.

8 Milton Viorst, *In the Shadow of the Prophet: The Struggle for the Soul of Islam* (New York: Anchor Books / Doubleday, 1998), 79.

9 Viorst, 78.

10 Viorst, 78.

11 Morey, 71.

12 Cooper, 104.

13 Ibid., 105.

14 Virost, 78, quoting Peters, *Muhammad*, 23.

15 Alan Jones, Introduction to the *Koran* (Rutland, VT: Charles E. Tuttle Co. Inc., 1994), xi–xii.

16 Armstrong, 3.

17 Marc Van De Mieroop explains that in ancient cultures this was popular. For instance, each city in Sumer had a main deity associated with it. Nippur was associated with the deity Enlil, Ur with Nanna, and Girsu with Ningirsu. It was the same all over the ancient world, except among the Jews and Christians who served only one God. *The Ancient Mesopotamian City* (Oxford, England: Oxford University Press, 1999), 46.

18 Robert Morey, *The Islamic Invasion: Confronting the World's Fastest Growing Religion* (Eugene, OR: Harvest House Publishers, 1992), 50. He refers to Alfred Guillaume, *Islam* (London: Penguin Books, 1954), 6.

19 Viorst, 80.

Chapter 5

1 Hurgronji, *Mohammedanism* (Westport, CT: Hyperion Press, 1981), 46.

2 Cooper, 106.

3 Cooper, 268.

4 Morey, 80.

5 Ibid., 106–107.

6 Cooper, 108.

7 Morey, 83.

8 Tor Andrae, *Mohammad: The Man and His Faith* (Mineola, NY: Dover Publications, Inc.; 1936, 2000), 145.

9 Morey, 178–190.

10 Armstrong, 55.

11 Mojdeh Bayat and Mohammad Ali Jamnia, *Tales from the Land of the Sufis* (Boston, MA: Shambhala Publications, Inc., 2001), 10
12 *World Magazine*, "Islamic worldview and how it differs from Christianity", October 27, 2001, 15.

Chapter 6

1 Armstrong, 24.
2 Andrae, 169.
3 Ibid., 170.
4 Cooper, 210.
5 Ruqaiyyah Maqsood, *Teach Yourself Islam* (Lincolnwood, IL: NTC/Contemporary Publishing, 1994), 22.
6 Ibid., 163.
7 Maqsood, 23.
8 Weiss, 19.
9 Ibid., 20.
10 Lewis, 296–297.
11 Armstrong, 44.
12 Cooper, 211.
13 Armstrong, 53.
14 *World Magazine*, Ibid.
15 Lewis, 309–310.
16 Cooper, 217.
17 John R. Hinnells, editor, *A Handbook of Living Religions* (New York, NY: Penguin Books, 1987), 129.
18 Bayat and Jamnia, 19–20.
19 Ron Carlson and Ed Decker, *Fast Facts on False Religions* (Eugene, OR: Harvest House Publishers, 1994), 72.
20 Tim Dowley, editor, *Eerdman's Handbook to The History of Christianity,* 270.
21 Armstrong, 95.
22 Lewis quoting Professor Gabrieli, 116–117.
23 Cooper, 214.
24 Armstrong, Ibid.
25 Lewis analyzes Ibn Khaldun's thoughts, who was considered the greatest of Arab historians from the fourteenth century, 203. Cooper also emphasizes Ibn Khaldun's views of the Seljuks, Mamluks, Mongols and Ottomans, as well as later historians confirming his opinions, 168.
26 Viorst, 215–217.
27 Stephen Neill, *Crisis in Belief* (London: Hodder and Stoughton, 1984), 61.

Chapter 7

1 Weiss, 29.
2 Maqsood, 45–46.

3 Halverson, 107.
4 Maqsood, 58.
5 Halverson, 107.
6 Weiss, 37.
7 John Renard, *Seven Doors To Islam: Spirituality and the Religious Life of Muslims* (Berkeley, CA: University of California Press, 1996), 39.
8 Weiss, 36.
9 Cooper, 127.
10 John Kelsay, *Islam and War: A Study in Comparative Ethics* (Louisville, KY: Westminister / John Knox Press, 1993), 34.
11 Weiss, 39.
12 Viorst, 16.
13 Bernard Lewis, *Wall Street Journal*, "Jihad vs. Crusade", New York, NY, September 27, 2001.
14 Koranic references will vary by several verses on one side or the other based on the version being used. This verse is taken from the Koran translated by J. M. Rodwell, and edited by Alan Jones of Oxford.
15 Fritz Ridenour, *So What's the Difference?* (Ventura, CA: Regal Books, 2001), 79.
16 Ridenour says the Koran lists 28 prophets, 80. Yet, Maqsood, who is a Muslim, indicates that there are 26 prophets mentioned in the Koran. These include biblical prophets such as Noah, Abraham, Moses, John the Baptists, and Jesus. But, there are three, Hud, Salih, and Shu'aib that are not from the biblical source. Their lives and origins are apparently unknown. Maqsood, 37.
17 Armstrong, 8.
18 Annemarie Schimmel and Abdoljavad Falaturi, *We Believe in One God* (New York, NY: The Seabury Press, 1979), 85.
19 Halverson says 80 %, 105. Yet, Cooper estimates that 90 % of Islam are Sunni, 179. Since both works are current, the statistics used come from different sources possibly employing varying standards. All the sources I researched used 10 % for the Shiites. Add to this the Sufi and many other little sects within Islam and I think 80 % for the Sunni is probably nearer the mark.
20 Maqsood, 109.
21 Cooper, 181.
22 Weiss, 68.
23 Maqsood, 24–25.
24 Weiss, Ibid.
25 Bayat and Jamnia, 11.
26 J. Dudley Woodberry, editor, *Muslims & Christians on the Emmaus Road* (Monrovia, CA: MARC Publications, 1989), 49.
27 Viorst, 142. He contends that both Jewish and Christian law lost much their social role because they were in cultures dominated by secular government,

such as Rome. Islamic law orients the faith to the past and keys Muslim society into an idyllic seventh century time of the Prophet. Muslim utopia is historic rather than spiritual in nature.

28 Imam Khomeini, *Islamic Government* "Program for the Establishment of an Islamic Government", in Iman Khomeini (tr. Hamid Algar), *Islam and Revolution: Writings and Declarations* (London: KRI, 1981), 137–138.

29 Lewis, 392.

30 Viorst, 174, 202.

31 Devi Asmarani, *Straight Times Indonesian Bureau,* "Syariah law? Jakarta offers new criminal code instead", October 19, 2001.

32 Viorst, 20

Chapter 8

1 *The Concise Encyclopedia of Islam*, edited by Cyril Classe (London: Stacey International, 1989), 230.

2 Morey cites examples of Koranic versions, textual problems, and a cover-up stories, chap. 9.

3 *The Oxford Dictionary of World Religions*, Edited by John Bowker (Oxford: Oxford University Press, 1997), 786.

4 Arthur Jeffrey, *The Foreign Vocabulary of the Quran* (Baroda: Oriental Institute, 1938), no. 79.

5 J. M. Rodwell, *The Koran*, notes, 448.

6 Ibid, 500.

7 Anne Cooper, 78.

8 Alan Jones, Introduction to *The Koran* (Rutland, VT: Charles E. Tuttle Co., Inc., 1995), xx.

9 Alan Jones, Introduction to *The Koran*, xiii.

10 Canon Sell, *Studies in Islam* (London: Diocesan Press, 1928), 208.

11 John McClintock and James Strong, *Cyclopedia of Biblical Theological, and Ecclesiastical Literature* (Baker Book House, 1981), V: 152.

12 Viorst notes that after a tumultuous battle Orthodox Islam won the battle against Mu'tazilism. The teachings of the dissident theologians offered a free will view of life, but Orthodox Islam denied it and offered fatalism, 87–88.

13 *The Oxford Dictionary of World Religions*, 786.

14 Quoted by Professor H. A. Gibb in *Mohammedanism: An Historical Survey*, 37.

15 Ali Dashti, *23 Years: A Study of the Prophetic Career of Mohammad* (London: George Allen & Unwin, 1985), 28.

16 Alan Jones, Introduction to *The Koran*, xxv.

17 John Renard, 11–13.

18 John Kelsay, *Islam and War: A Study in Comparative Ethics* (Louisville, KY: Westminster / John Knox Press, 1993), 34–35.

19 Viorst, 100.

Chapter 9

1 Gulshan Esther, *The Torn Veil* (Fort Washington, PA: Published by Christian Literature Crusade, 1998), 61.

2 See Geoffrey Parrinder for a complete listing, *Jesus in the Qur'an* (New York, NY: Oxford University Press, 1977), 18–20.

3 *The Oxford Dictionary of World Religions*, 692.

4 Hans Küng, *et al., Christianity and the World Religions: Paths to Dialogue with Islam, Hinduism, and Buddhism* (London: Collins, 1986).

5 Note in *The Koran*, 438.

6 George Braswell, *Islam: Its Prophets, Peoples, Politics and Power* (Nashville, TN: Broadman & Holman Publishers, 1996), 279.

7 S. F. Fleming, *Gate Breakers: Answering Cults and World Religions with Prayer, Love and Witnessing* (Seattle, WA: Selah Publishing, 1998), 34. In that book, I spend a chapter on the authenticity of the Old and New Testaments.

8 Braswell, 279.

9 Noor ul Haq, *Al-Masih: The Anointed One* (Minneapolis, MN: Center for Ministry to Muslims, 1996), 26.

10 David A. Hubbard, *Does the Bible Really Work?* (Waco, TX: Word Books, 1972), 31–32.

11 Noor ul Haq, *The Mercy of Allah* (Minneapolis, MN: Center for Ministry to Muslims, 1996), 7.

12 Braswell, 282.

13 Braswell, 283.

14 Mahmoud M. Ayoub, *Muslim World*, "Toward an Islamic Christology", "The Death of Jesus: reality or delusion", lxx, (1980), 116.

15 Harry Morin, *Responding to Muslims* (Springfield, MO: Center for Ministry to Muslims, 2000), 61.

16 John R. W. Stott, *Christianity Today*, "God on the Gallows", January 27, 1987, 30.

17 In Ephesians 6, Paul explains that the armor of God includes the belt of truth, breastplate of righteousness, shoes of the gospel of peace, shield of faith, helmet of salvation, and the sword of the Spirit, which is the word of God. Associated with this armor is the incessant need for prayer.

Chapter 10

1 Jeff Taylor, *Charisma Magazine*, "I Must Get a Bible", October 1997, 53.

2 John Foxe, *Foxe's Book of Martyrs* (Springfield, PA: Whitaker House, 1891). In chapter one, Foxe gives an account of all the first disciples and their consequent deaths as martyrs.

3 The Watchman Expositor, *2000 Index of Cults and Religions*, (Birmingham, AL: Published by Watchman Fellowship, Inc., 2000), Volume 17, No. 1, 28.

4 S. F. Fleming, 8.

5 Andree Seu, *World Magazine*, "Multi-culti widowhood", September 8, 2001,

53.

6 Weiss, 50.

7 Andrew Rippin and Jan Knappert, editors and translators, *Textual Sources for the Study of Islam* (Chicago: University of Chicago Press, 1990), 196.

8 Rashid, 128–129.

9 Ibid, 130.

10 Yossef Bodansky, *Bin Laden: The Man Who Declared War on America* (Roseville, CA: Prima Publishing / Random House, Inc., 2001), 36.

11 Ahmad Khomeini, *Kayhan,* Tehran, January 11, 1992—as reported by Mohammad Mohaddessin, *Islamic Fundamentalism: The New Global Threat* (Washington, DC: Seven Locks Press, 1993), 39.

12 Ibid, 207.

13 Armstrong, 175.

14 Bodansky, 275.

15 John Kelsay, 95–97.

16 John Kelsay, 100.

17 Ibid, 318.

18 Michael Elliot, *Time Magazine*, "Hate Club", November 12, 2001, 61.

19 Bodansky, 338–339.

20 Rashid, 93.

21 Bodansky, 387–389.

22 Armstrong, 180, 182.

23 David Landes, *The Wealth and Poverty of Nations* (London: Abacus, 1999), 509.

24 Rashid, 83.

25 Bodansky, 340.

26 Internet News Release from Christian Aid, info@christian.org. There are various Christian Aid sites on the web in the United States or Canada.

27 Ibid, 412–413.

28 Reuters News Story from the Internet, "Woman to Face Death by Stoning for Adultery", October 19, 2001.

29 Ed Decker, a paper entitled *Understanding Islam: The Mystery Religion*, November 2001, 9.

30 Landes, 414.

31 Ronald Segal, *Islam's Black Slaves* (New York, NY: Farrar, Straus, and Giroux, 2001), 202–203.

32 Ibid, 204, 218–221.

33 *Maranatha Christian Journal*, "Ministry Redeems More Than 2,000 Slaves", July 11, 1999. www. Mcjonline.com/news/news3228.htm

Chapter 11

1 William Miller, *A Christian Response to Islam* (Phillipsburg, NJ: Presbyterian and Reformed Publishing Company, 1976), 125–126.

2 Wes Daughenbaugh, *The Heart God Hears* (Chelalis, WA: Gospel Net Ministries, 1996), 114.
3 David Shibley, *A Force in the Earth: The Charismatic Renewal and World Evangelism* (Altamonte Springs, FL: Creation House, 1990), 137.
4 E. M. Bounds, *Purpose in Prayer* (New York, NY: Fleming H. Revell Company, 1920), 79.
5 *Light the Window* Video, Produced by CBN International, 977 Centerville, Turnpike, Virginia Beach, VA, 23464, 1995.
6 *Window Watchman II*, compiled and edited by Beverly Pegues (Colorado Springs, CO: Published by Christian Information Network, 1997), 10.
7 AD2000 & Beyond Website. www. Ad2000.org/ "Praying Through the Window IV: Light the Window."
8 Ed Silvoso, *That None Should Perish: How to Reach Entire Cities for Christ Through Prayer Evangelism* (Ventura, CA: Regal Books, 1994, 271.
9 Jane Rumph, *Stories from the Front Lines: Power Evangelism in Today's World* (Grand Rapids: MI: Chosen Books, 1996, 85–87.
10 Ibid, 210.
11 Ibid, 312, 317.
12 Arabic Bible Outreach. www. Arabicbible.com "testimonial page".
13 Jane Rumph, chapter nine.
14 Ibid, 244–245.
15 Jane Rumph, 229.
16 S. D. Gordon, *Quiet Talks on Prayer* (New York, NY: Grosset & Dunlap (Fleming H. Revell), 1941), 28, 35.
17 Chrysostom as quoted in E. M. Bounds, *Purpose in Prayer* (New York, NY: Fleming H. Revell Company, 1920), 32.
18 *Charisma Magazine*, "Escape from False Gods", (October, 1997), 59.
19 Steve Sjogren, *Conspiracy of Kindness* (Ann Arbor, MI: Servant Publications, 1993), 22–23.
20 Watchman II, 231.
21 Arabia Bible Outreach Ministry, Internet, "testimonial page".
22 Jane Rumph, 230.
23 William Montgomery Watt, 105.
24 *Window Watchman II*, 324.
25 William Miller, 113–114.
26 Copper, 293–294.

Chapter 12

1 Internet, Arabic Christian Personal Pages, Athanasios's page. www.arabicbible.com.
2 Paul G. and Frances F. Hiebert, *Case Studies in Missions* (Grand Rapids, MI: Baker Book House, 1987), 223–225.

3 Sermon at the House of the Lord Church; Oldtown, Idaho; January 14, 1996.

4 I used Ed Silvoso's categories of strongholds and applied them to Islamic deception. Ed Silvoso, *That None Should Perish: How to Reach Entire Cities for Christ through Prayer Evangelism* (Ventura, CA: Regal Books, 1994), 158–168.

5 Nadia Mustafa, *Time Magazine,* "After 50 Years, a Muslim Split", November 5, 2001, 18.

6 CBS, *60 Minutes*, Internet site, "Cheers to Jeers in Kuwait", November 18, 2001.

7 From Reuters on the Internet, MSNBC, "Attack on Christian church killed 16", October 29, 2001.

8 Lindy Warren, *Charisma Magazine*, "German Evangelist Takes Gospel to Pakistan", December 2001, 24–25.

9 Phil Parshall, 206.

10 Armstrong, 30.

GLOSSARY

Abbasid Dynasty. (AD 750–935) Dominating from Baghdad, it was known as the golden age of Islam.

Abdallah Ibn Jahsh. Team leader sent by Muhammad in the Nakha Raid.

'Abd al-Malik. Caliph who built the Dome of the Rock from AD 689–691.

'Abdulla bin Ubai bin Salul. Mistakenly accused Muhammad's wife, Aisha, of adultery and was executed.

Abdullah Azzam. Osama bin Laden's teacher and strong influence at King Abdul Aziz University in Jidda.

Abraham. Father of Isaac and Ishmael. Muslims, Jews, and Christians view Abraham as a patriarch.

Abu Bakr. First caliph after Muhammad's death.

Ahzab. Third battle between Muhammad and the Meccans. Muhammad was victorious.

Aisha. Considered to be Muhammad's favorite wife.

Al-Aqsa Mosque. Located in Jerusalem.

Alawites. Minor sect of Islam that believes women do not have souls.

al-intifada. Arabic term for shaking off illegitimate political rule.

Ali. Fourth caliph and husband of Muhammad's daughter, Fatima. Shiites consider descendents to be the true imams.

Allah. Islamic name for the God of Abraham. Original term referred to moon deity and head of the Arabic pantheon of gods.

Al-Lat. Primary goddess daughter of Allah.

Al-Manat. Goddess daughter of Allah. Had scissors by which she cut the threads of human fate.

Al-Masih Isa. Arabic for "Jesus the Messiah."

Al-Qaeda. Islamic terrorist network lead by Osama bin Laden.

Al-Rahman. Allah as the god of mercy and compassion.

Al-Uzza. Goddess daughter of Allah. Literally translated as "most powerful."

Anwar Sadat. Egyptian president who started peace talks with Israel in 1977, offered aid to the fledgling Afghani resistance in 1980, and was assassinated by Islamic fundamentalists in October 1981.

Arab. Any member of a Semitic people located in the southern Arabian Peninsula, or those from an Arabic-speaking group.

Ariel Sharon. Prime minister of Israel in 2001. Offered support to the U.S. after the September 11th attack.

Aus. Arab tribe that inhabited Medina during Muhammad's ascension to power.

ayas. Arabic term that means "signs" or "verses" in the Koran.

Badr. First battle between Muhammad and the Meccans.

Baha'u'llah. Nineteenth century co-founder of Baha'ism who claimed to be the return of the twelfth imam of Shiite tradition.

caliph. "Rightly guided one," used to indicate successor of Muhammad.

dar-al-Harb. "House of war," referring to all territories outside of dar-al-Islam.

dar-al-Islam. "House of Islam" or "house of peace."

deen. Religious obligations as directed by the beliefs of Islam.

Dome of the Rock. Mosque built in Jerusalem in AD 691 to mark the spot where Muslims believe Muhammad began his night journey to heaven.

Eblis. Koranic name for Satan prior to his fall.

Egyptian Islamic Jihad. Egyptian fundamentalist groups responsible for terrorism.

Fahd. King of Saudi Arabia who drew criticism from Osama bin Laden and consequently revoked bin Laden's citizenship.

faqih. Jurist or expert in Islamic law.

fatrah. Intermission in Muhammad's writing of the Koran.

fatwas. The religious decisions and decrees of Islam.

Fifth Column. Name for Islamic terrorists cells within the United States.

fundamentalism. Form of religious extremism.

Gabriel. Intermediary angel that Islamic tradition says Allah used to reveal the Koran to Muhammad.

Hadith. Sacred collection of Islamic sayings and traditions.

Hagar. Mother of Ishmael.

Hanafites. Liberal school of Islamic law.

Hanbalites. Dogmatic school of Islamic law.

Hasan al-Banna. Founder of the Muslim Brotherhood in Egypt, 1928.

Hattin. Battle where Saladin defeated the Crusaders in 1187.

Hosni Mubarak. Egyptian president who tried to route Egyptian terrorist groups after the assassination of his predecessor, Anwar Sadat.

Hamas. An Islamic resistance movement in Jordan.

Hanifs. Monotheistic group of Muhammad's contemporaries who considered themselves the spiritual descendents of Abraham.

Hashim. Muhammad's clan in the Quraysh tribe.

Hezbollah. Lebanese terrorist organization, the "Party of God."

Hijra. Migration of Muhammad's followers from Mecca to Medina that marks the start of the Muslim calendar.

hajj. A pilgrimage to Mecca; one of the five pillars of Islam.

imam. Religious leader of a mosque; also refers to the "beliefs" of Islam.

Imamites. Name of the Twelver Shiite sect.

Injil. Arabic term for the gospels of the Bible.

intifada. (Also *al-intifada.*) Specifies the clash between Palestinian Arabs and Israelis.

Isa. Arabic name for Jesus.

Ishmael. Son of Abraham who fathered the Bedouins and Arabs.

Ishmailites. Name of the Sevener Shiite sect.

Islam. The religion founded by Muhammad. Literally means "submission."

Islamic revivalism. Politically correct term for Islamic fundamentalism.

Jafarites. Shiite school of Islamic law.

jihad. Struggle or effort; the greater is a personal inner battle while the lesser is an outer domestic battle trying to extend the dar-al-Islam into the dar-al-Harb.

jinn. Genies or demons referred to in the Koran.

Kabah. Shrine in Mecca that stands as the center of Muslim worship.

Kainuka. Arabic tribe in Medina during Muhammad's ascension to power.

Khadijah. Muhammad's first wife.

Khatami, Mohammed. President of Iran since 1997.

Khomeini, Ayatollah. Religious revolutionary who overthrew the Shaw of Iran in 1979.

Koran. The holiest book of Islam. Literally means "recitation," referring to Muhammad's revelations from the angel Gabriel.

Malikites. Islamic school of law in Medina during Muhammad's reign.

Mauritania. African country in which slavery still exists under Islamic rule.

mawalis. Literally "clients," referring to Islam converts.

Mecca. The holiest city of Islam; Muhammad's birthplace.

Medina. City where Muhammad came to power, waged his attacks against Mecca, and finally died.

Moghal Empire. (AD 1526–1827) Located in India.

Mohammad Omar. Founded the Taliban in the mid 1990s and lead the Afghani resistance against the United States in 2001.

Mossad. Israel's secret intelligence agency.

Mu'âwiya. First caliph of the Umayyad Dynasty.

Muhammad. Founder of Islam, author of the Koran, and considered in Islamic tradition as the greatest prophet of all times.

Muhammad al-Madhi. Twelfth and final imam of the Shiite movement; known as the "hidden imam."

Mujahideen. Islamic warriors that formed the Afghani resistance against Russia in the 1980s; literally "those who wage the jihad."

Muslim. Believer of Islam; literally "one who is submitted" to Allah.

Muslim Brotherhood. Twentieth-century Egyptian fundamentalist group started by Hasan al-Banna.

Mu'tazilites. Group of ninth-century theologians who challenged the Koran as eternal and uncreated.

Nakha Raid. First raid that Muhammad authorized.

Nasser, Abdul. Egyptian ruler who in 1956 prompted the first of several wars with Israel.

Osama bin Laden. Leader and organizer of the Al-Qaeda terrorist network and primary suspect for numerous atrocities, including the World Trade Center attack on September 11, 2001.

Ottoman Empire. Began in AD 1380 with vestiges of lasting until after WWI.

Pahlevi, Muhammad Reza. Pro-Western Shaw of Iran ousted in 1979 by the Ayatollah Khomeini.

Palestinian Liberation Organization (PLO). Terrorist organization founded by Yassir Arafat to battle Israel in the intifada.

Pope Urban II. Proclaimed the need for the first crusade in AD 1095.

qiblah. The direction Muslims face during prayer.

Quraysh. Tribe in Mecca to which Muhammad belonged.

rakahs. The traditional eight-step Islamic prayer that is repeated five times a day.

Ramadan. Islamic holy month set aside for fasting during sunlight hours.

Saddam Hussein. Leader of Iraq who was responsible for the invasion of Kuwait in the early 1990s.

Safavid Empire. (AD 1503–1722) Formed as a strong union between Turkish tribesmen and Persian bureaucratic leaders.

Saladin. Islamic leader who defeated the crusaders and recaptured Jerusalem in AD 1187.

salat. Arabic term for "prayer."

Satanic verses. Controversial suras that were included in the Koran to permit worship of Allah's three goddess daughters. Considered by some to be led by a deception from Satan, especially when the verses were later changed.

sawm. Term for the month of fasting during Ramadan.

Seljuk Turks. (AD 990–1118) Turkish family that ruled and defeated the Byzantines at the Battle of Manizkurt, 1071.

shahadah. The creed of Islam: "There is no god but Allah, and Muhammad is his messenger."

Shaitan. Arabic for "Satan."

Shafiites. The moderate school of Islamic law.

Shariah. The law of Islam; literally "the way."

Shiites. Radical Islamic sect that only recognize the caliphs who have descended from Ali.

shirk. Literally "blasphemy," as in associating other gods with Allah.

Sidrah-tree. The tree that is near God in paradise and beyond which no human and angel can pass.

Sudan. African country in which slavery still exists under Islamic rule.

sunnah (sunna). Islamic customs.

Sunnites. Orthodox sect of Islam that includes the largest percentage of Muslims.

Sufi. The more animistic and mystical Islamic sect.

sura. Chapters or portions of the Koran.

tasbih (subhah). Islamic prayer breads.

Tawrat. The Torah—first five books of the Old Testament.

Uhud. Muhammad's second battle with the Meccans.

ulema (ulama). Scholars and guardians of the legal and religious traditions of Islam.

Umar. The second caliph to succeed Abu Bakr.

Umayyad Dynasty. (AD 661–750) Replaced original caliphs and made Damascus the capital.

ummah. The community of Muslim believers.

Umm al-kittab. The Koran as the pre-existent tablet preserved in heaven.

'umra. The smaller pilgrimage to Mecca, often in lieu of the hajj.

Uthman. The third caliph who succeeded Umar.

Taliban. Islamic extremist group that ruled Afghanistan in the late 1990s.

Yathrib. The name of the city of Medina prior to Muhammad's rule.

Wahhabism. Extremist group founded by Muhammad ibn Abd al-Wahhab in the eighteenth century and linked to the House of Saud, from which came the present Saudi state.

Zabur. The Psalms.

Zaydites. Name of the Fiver Shiite sect of Islam.

zakat. Literally "alms"; one of the five pillars of Islam.

BIBLIOGRAPHY

AD 2000 & Beyond. "Praying through the Window IV: Light the Window." Internet: www.Ad2000.org/.Adherents.com/rel_USA.html#religions. Internet: "Statistics."

Andrae, Tor. *Mohammad: The Man and His Faith*. (Mineola, NY: Dover Publications, Inc.) 2000—reprint 1936.

Arabic Bible Outreach. Internet: www. Arabicbible.com. "Testimonial page."

Armstrong, Karen. *Islam: A Short History*. (New York: Random House) 2000.

Asmarani, Devi. "Syariah law? Jakarta offers new criminal code instead." *Straight Times Indonesian Bureau*. 19 October 2001.

Ayoub, Mahmoud M. "Toward an Islamic Christology." *Muslim World*. "The Death of Jesus: Reality or Delusion," 1980.

Backgrounder—Terrorism. Internet: www.Nsi.org/Library/Terrorism/facterr.html.

Barna, George. Internet: www.barna.org "Statistics."

Bayat, Mojdeh., and Mohammad Ali Jamnia. *Tales from the Land of the Sufis*. (Boston, MA: Shambhala Publications, Inc.) 2001.

Belz, Mindy. "We Are the World." *World Magazine*. (Asheville, NC) 22 September 2001.

Bin Laden, Osama. *World Islamic Front Statement*. Internet: Cornell University Web site. 23 February 1998.

Bodansky, Yossef. *Bin Laden: The Man Who Declared War on America*. (Roseville, CA: Prima Publishing / Random House, Inc.) 2001.

Booker, Richard. *Blow the Trumpet in Zion*. (Shippensburg, PA: Destiny Image Publishers) 1992.

Bounds, E. M. *Purpose in Prayer*. (New York, NY: Fleming H. Revell Company) 1920.

Braswell, George W. Jr. *Islam: Its Prophets, Peoples, Politics and Power.* (Nashville, TN: Broadman & Holman Publishers) 1996.

Burton, Dan. "Preparing for the War on Terrorism." Washington, D.C: Committee on Government Reform, 20 September 2001.

Carlson, Ron. Christian Ministries International. personal e-mail. (Eden Prairie, MN) 2001.

__________, and Ed Decker. *Fast Facts on False Religions.* (Eugene, OR: Harvest House Publishers) 1994.

CBS's *60 Minutes.* 25 November 2001.

__________ "Cheers to Jeers in Kuwait." CBS's *60 Minutes* Internet site: 18 November 2001.

Chronology of Terror. Internet: www.cnn.com, 12 September 2001.

Clarke, Adam. *Adam Clarke's Commentary on the Holy Bible.* (Grand Rapids, MI: Baker Book House) 1987.

Classe, Cyril. *The Concise Encyclopedia of Islam.* (London: Stacey International) 1989.

Cloud, John. "What Is Al-Qaeda Without Its Boss?" *Time Magazine.* (New York) 26 November 2001.

Cooper, Anne. *Ishmael My Brother: A Christian Introduction to Islam.* (Crowborough, East Sussex, Great Britain: MARC) 1997.

Daughenbaugh, Wes. *The Heart God Hears.* (Chelalis, WA: Gospel Net Ministries) 1996.

Eerdman's Handbook to the History of Christianity. (Grand Rapids, MI: Wm. B. Eerdman's Publishing Company) 1977.

Elliot, Michael. "Hate Club." *Time Magazine.* (New York) 12 November 2001.

Esposito, John L. *Islamic Threat: Myth or Reality?* third edition. (New York: Oxford University Press) 1999.

Esther, Gulshan. *The Torn Veil.* (Fort Washington, PA: Christian Literature Crusade) 1998.

Farrel, Elisabeth. "Escape from False Gods." *Charisma Magazine.* (Lake Mary, FL) October 1997.

Flinchbaugh , C. Hope. "Christian Workers from United States Remain Jailed in Afghanistan." *Charisma Magazine.* (Lake Mary, FL) December 2001.

Foxe, John. *Foxe's Book of Martyrs.* (Springfield, PA: Whitaker House) 1981.

Gordon, S. D. *Quiet Talks on Prayer.* (New York, NY: Grosset & Dunlap / Fleming H. Revell) 1941.

Greenberger, Robert S., and Alix Freedman. "Sergeant served U.S. and bin Laden." Intenet: MSNBC, 11 November 2001.

Guillaume, Alfred. *Islam.* (London: Penguin Books) 1954.

Hadith. Volume 1, Numbers 211, 345.

Hag, Noor ul. *The Mercy of Allah.* (Minneapolis, MN: Center for Ministry to Muslims) 1996.

Hinnells, John R. *A Handbook of Living Religions.* (New York, NY: Penguin Books) 1987.

Jones, Bob. "Morning of Terrors." *World Magazine*. (Asheville, NC) 18 September 2001.

Josephus: Complete Works. (Grand Rapids, MI: Kregel Publications) 1980.

Halverson, Dean. *The Compact Guide to World Religions*. (Minneapolis, MN: Bethany House Publishers) 1996.

Harden, Donald. *The Phoenicians: Ancient Peoples and Places*. (New York, NY: Frederick A. Praeger, Publisher) 1963.

Hiebert, Paul G. and Frances F. *Case Studies in Missions*. (Grand Rapids, MI: Baker Book House) 1987.

Hurgronji. *Mohammedanism*. (Westport, CT: Hyperion Press) 1981.

Index of Cults and Religions. (The Watchman Expositor. Birmingham, AL: Watchman Fellowship, Inc.) 2000.

Kaplan, David E., and Kevin Whitelaw. "The CEO of Terror Inc." *U.S. News & World Report*. (New York) 1 October 2001.

Kelsay, John. *Islam and War: A Study in Comparative Ethics*. (Louisville, KY: Westminster / John Knox Press) 1993.

Khomeini. *Islam and Revolution: Writings and Declarations*. (London: KRI) 1981.

Koran. (Rutland, VT: Charles E. Tuttle Co. Inc.) 1994.

Küng, Hans. *Christianity and the World Religions: Paths to Dialogue with Islam, Hinduism, and Buddhism*. (London: Collins) 1986.

Lewis, Bernard. *Islam in History: Ideas, People, and Events in the Middle East*. (Chicago, IL: Open Court) 1993.

__________. "Jihad vs. Crusade." *The Wall Street Journal*. (New York) 27 September 2001.

Light the Window Video. (Virginia Beach, VA: CBN International) 1995.

McClintock, John, and James Strong. *Cyclopedia of Biblical Theological, and Ecclesiastical Literature*. (Baker Book House) 1981.

Maqsood, Ruqaiyyah. *Teach Yourself Islam*. (Lincolnwood, IL: NTC/Contemporary Publishing) 1994.

Maranatha Christian Journal. "Ministry Redeems More Than 2,000 Slaves." Internet: www.Mcjonline.com/news/news3228.htm, 11 July 1999.

Mather, George A., and Larry A. Nichols. *Dictionary of Cults, Sects, Religions and the Occult*. (Grand Rapids, MI: Zondervan Publishing House) 1993.

Merriam-Webster Thesaurus. (Springfield, MA: Merriam-Webster Inc.) 1989.

Mikkelson, Barbara and David P. "False Prophecy." Internet: www.snopes.com.

Miller, William. *A Christian Response to Islam*. (Phillipsburg, NJ: Presbyterian and Reformed Publishing Company) 1976.

Minor, David. "Strongholds." (Oldtown, ID) Taped message at House of the Lord. 14 January 1996.

Mohaddessin, Mohammad. *Islamic Fundamentalism: The New Global Threat*. (Washington, DC: Seven Locks Press) 1993.

Mordecai, Victor. *Is Fanatic Islam A Global Threat?* (Taylors, SC) 1997.

Morey, Robert. *The Islamic Invasion: Confronting the World's Fastest Growing Religion*. (Eugene, OR: Harvest House Publishers) 1992.

Morin, Harry. *Responding to Muslims.* (Springfield, MO: Center for Ministry to Muslims) 2000.

MSNBC. "Attack on Christian church killed 16." Internet site: www.nbc.com. 29 October 2001.

MSNBC. "Israel Fires Missiles Near Arafat Headquarters." Internet site: www.nbc.com. 3 December 2001.

Musk, Bill A. *Passionate Believing.* (Tunbridge Wells: Monarch Publications) 1992.

Mustafa, Nadia. "After 50 Years, a Muslim Split." *Time Magazine.* (New York) 5 November 2001.

Neill, Stephen. *Crisis in Belief.* (London: Hodder and Stoughton) 1984.

Olasky, Marvin. "Islamic worldview and how it differs from Christianity." *World Magazine.* (Asheville, NC) 27 October 2001.

Oxford Dictionary of World Religions. (Oxford: Oxford University Press) 1997.

Parrinder, Geoffrey. *Jesus in the Qur'an.* (New York, NY: Oxford University Press) 1977.

Parshall, Phil. *The Cross and the Crescent.* (Wheaton, IL: Tyndale House Publishers, Inc.) 1989.

Profile of Osama bin Laden. Internet: Anti-Defamation League, www.adl.org/terrorism_America/bin_l.asp.

Random House Webster's College Dictionary. (New York: Random House) 1992.

Rashid, Ahmed. *Militant Islam, Oil, & Fundamentalism in Central Asia.* (New Haven: Yale University Press) 2001.

Renard, John. *Seven Doors To Islam: Spirituality and the Religious Life of Muslims.* (Berkeley, CA: University of California Press) 1996.

Ridenour, Fritz. *So What's the Difference?* (Ventura, CA: Regal Books) 2001.

Rippin, Andrew, and Jan Knappert. *Textual Sources for the Study of Islam.* (Chicago: University of Chicago Press) 1990.

Rumph, Jane. *Stories from the Front Lines: Power Evangelism in Today's World.* (Grand Rapids: MI: Chosen Books) 1996.

Schimmel, Annemarie, and Abdoljavad Falaturi. *We Believe in One God.* (New York, NY: The Seabury Press) 1979.

Segal, Ronald. *Islam's Black Slaves.* (New York, NY: Farrar, Straus, and Giroux) 2001.

Sell, Canon. *Studies in Islam.* (London: Diocesan Press) 1928.

Shibley, David. *A Force in the Earth: The Charismatic Renewal and World Evangelism.* (Altamonte Springs, FL: Creation House) 1990.

Silvoso, Ed. *That None Should Perish: How to Reach Entire Cities for Christ through Prayer Evangelism.* (Ventura, CA: Regal Books) 1994.

Sjogren, Steve. *Conspiracy of Kindness.* (Ann Arbor, MI: Servant Publications) 1993.

Smith, Wendell. *God Can Still Bless America.* (Kirkland, WA: Publication of the City Church) 2001.

Stott, John R. W. "God on the Gallows." *Christianity Today.* 27 January 1987.

Strong, James. *The New Strong's Exhaustive Concordance of the Bible.* (Nashville, TN: Thomas Nelson Publishers) 1995.

Taylor, Jeff. "I Must Get a Bible." *Charisma Magazine.* (Lake Mary, FL) October 1997.

The Relativities and the Rhetoric. CNN's "Special Report." 14 October 2001, 8:00 pm PST.

"Time line on Osama bin Laden's Life." Internet: www.cnn.com.

Tyrangiel, Josh. "Did You Hear About?" *Time Magazine.* 8 October 2001.

Us-israel.org. Internet: "Relationship between U.S. and Israel."

__________. "Timeline."

__________. Selection from *The Los Angeles Times.* 20 September 2001.

Vahanian, Gabriel. *Wait without Idols.* (New York: George Braziller) 1964.

Van De Mieroop, Marc. *The Ancient Mesopotamian City.* (Oxford, England: Oxford University Press) 1999.

Viorst, Milton. *In the Shadow of the Prophet: The Struggle for the Soul of Islam.* (New York: Anchor Books / Doubleday) 1998.

Wagner, Clarence H. Jr. "Between a Rock and a Holy Site." *Christianity Today.* 5 February 2001.

Warren, Lindy. "German Evangelist Takes Gospel to Pakistan." *Charisma Magazine* (Lake Mary, FL) December 2001.

Watt, William Montgomery. *Muslim—Christian Encounters: Perceptions and Misperceptions.* (New York: Routledge) 1991.

Weiss, Walter M. *Islam: An Illustrated Historical Overview.* (Hauppauge, NY: Barron's Educational Series) 2000.

Window Watchman II. (Colorado Springs, CO: Christian Information Network) 1997.

Woodberry, J. Dudley. *Muslims & Christians on the Emmaus Road.* (Monrovia, CA: MARC Publications) 1989.

To order additional copies of

ISLAM
and New Global Realities
The Roots of Islamic Fundamentalism